Facing a Bottle of Henny

A College Coming-Of-Age Tale

Zander Tsadwa

DISCLAIMER: Listen fam. I don't *really* owe anyone when it comes to the accuracy of these stories. It's a memoir; it's based on *my* memories. But luckily for you, the reader, and the people included in this wonderful book, I have hella integrity.

Some events are compressed or omitted for the purpose of narrative cohesiveness. Even if you're upset about the exclusion of that one cool thing we did that one time, trust me, the mess of my first drafts can't beat the cleaner version of my college experience in your hands right now. I can also tell you what *is* in the book is as close to the truth of my experience as possible.

Extensive interviews of people in and around the referenced events have greatly refined my recollection of said events and the characters in them. No events are fabricated, no real names are used without permission, and the dialogue is made up of direct quotes and appropriate recreations. Documents that were created at the time of the events in question including (but not limited to) emails, screenshots, and personal journal entries were heavily referenced in the retelling of these stories. Also, all unfavorable descriptions and opinions of events and entities are included only to add significance my reflections.

In short, I'm not out here exaggerating, lying, or being petty for fun. I promise.

Edited by Jadea Washington and Josh Plattner
Book cover design by Sunita Dharod

To my family, friends, and the University of St. Thomas community

Contents

Pregame (Preface)

•••

To face something in the informal sense is to directly con-sume it. To take something in with no assistance. College is a time where many people "face" things: blunts, joints, liquor straight from the bottle. Normal shit. It is also a time where many face, in the formal sense, challenges on the way to becoming real adults. As a young brown-skinned kid groomed in diverse public schools, the challenges of attending a private Catholic university were numer-ous. Among those challenges was finding acceptance in a communi-ty that only cared about me in principle, not practice.

My struggle to be acknowledged on campus echoed the sto-ries of Black American artists that moved to France in search of ac-ceptance in the early twentieth century. Along with Black soldiers stationed there, Black artists were surprisingly well received by the French. According to Dr. Emory Tolbert of Howard University, jazz and blues music filled up Parisian clubs in the years between World War I and II. The drink of choice at these venues? Cognac. The connection between the 'yac and Black folk was decades old by the end of WWII, a time where French spirit brands started placing ads with Black models in the iconic magazines *Ebony* and *Jet*.

As major brands of cognac battled for the loyalty of Black Americans during the Civil Rights Movement, Hennessy did more than keep up. According to Noel Hankin, Hennessy's former Vice President of Multicultural Marketing, Hennessy didn't just target Black folk in advertising: they invested in them. William Jay Schieffelin, the company's founding president, was an influential supporter of Booker T. Washington's Tuskegee Institute in its early days. He also played a major role in founding the National Urban League, one of America's oldest civil rights organizations. Along with behind-the-scenes work, Hennessy's long history of Black advocates starts at Olympic medalist Herb Douglass and continues today with the dozens of hip-hop artists who frequently praise it, including current brand ambassador Nasir "Nas" Jones.

Cognac isn't Kool-Aid. It's not sugary, nor easy to drink. But the special history Black folk have with Hennessy makes it sweet enough. Much like drinking Hennessy is unique to Black Americans, there's a certain bittersweetness unique to the college experiences of black and brown students across the nation. The sting of downing Henny, followed by exuberant cheers from friends, is akin to the sting of racism and social exclusion on campus being rewarded by the applause of your peers when you triumphantly graduate. In both cases, an acerbic experience becomes a lighthearted buzz, a sense of accomplishment that wouldn't be as satisfying had you not went through something unpleasant to get it.

Before we hop into the wildness of *Facing a Bottle of Henny*, know that I truly enjoyed my time at the University of St. Thomas.

When you're placed in an unfamiliar environment, your choices are to resist and not learn a thing, or to adapt and grow in it. As a first-generation American, a first-generation college student, and a Black kid from inner-city St. Paul, Minnesota, the truth of my college experience was an entertaining middle ground between those two choices.

I grew to enjoy being the odd one out because it forced me to believe the power I had in simply existing. If you limit your world to those who think and act like you, there isn't as much pressure on you to radiate. Your presence feels accounted for, you don't have to stand out. But to be surrounded on all sides by people who think Ethiopians speak "Ethiopian," or people who don't understand that college isn't a guarantee for everyone, I had to be sure in myself. Once I started thinking of my difference as an asset rather than a liability, my presence grew. I radiated. Melanin and all, St. Thomas forced me to glow from the inside out.

That being said, getting to that point was a mission. Maintaining that glow was just as tough. The struggle was harder on some of my friends than it was for me, and it wasn't just the subtle, constant racial tension. It was walking amongst thousands of people who seemed to already know each other, but had to test us. It was the concerned looks we would receive at a party for trying to dance with people we didn't know as if they weren't there to socialize, making us feel dumb for trying[1]. It was the blank expressions we got from other Black students after saying, "Wassup," only to see them in the gym or at the cafeteria with standoffish White people.

No matter how familiar campus became to me, I was always a stranger. Barely anyone was going to reach out to make that process easier for me. I could use terms like "PWI," "microaggression," and other choice social justice verbiage to explain my experience at St. Thomas. That language is necessary in the fight to validate experiences such as mine. But for what I'm about to drop on you, it's too sterile.

There will be many serious things I bring to your attention, but a lot of this shit is also hilarious. I want to laugh about closeted racism as much as I want to address it. I want to detail my experiences with White girls and weed as much as I want to psychoanalyze my peers. I want to blow your mind with unique observations on the intersection of race and class in Minnesota, *and* tell you about the party bus that went so hard it almost killed a friend of mine.

I could frame this book as a story about a young brown boy who barely survived to tell the tale of a backwards private Catholic school in Minnesota. Or, I can sink into this couch and type up an *adventure*. One that touches on the good, the bad, the beautiful, and the ugly of the journey to adulthood in a strange college bubble. It was a weird place where kids got blackout drunk next to a building full of priests in-training. It was also a beautiful place where students from faraway countries helped me see the United States in a glorious new light. Most importantly, it was a place where kids who felt powerless due to their difference made their difference powerful with a smile and some courage.

This adventure has a variety of checkpoints. Like a musical playlist with an overarching theme, you can read this book straight through, or pick and choose the tracks (chapters) that seem most interesting. Whichever way you go about it, you will be consuming sharp, candid thoughts and stories at every turn. Whether the taste shocks, humors, irritates, or overwhelms you, I hope this colorful blend of reflections leaves you with a pleasant buzz once you're done.

Ladies and gentlemen, nervous faculty and staff members, jaded college seniors, overwhelmed freshmen, my parents, the homies, curious Black individuals, nosey "progressive" White folk, and the rest of y'all, let's begin *Facing a Bottle of Henny*.

1

You See Me And You Don't

•••

Staring off in the distance while walking by a stranger is proper etiquette in any real city center. It's like the choice most make to shoo away a person asking for change to get on the bus. Perfectly acceptable behavior, not rude or antisocial. You can't assume someone is a bigoted jerk for not greeting you. The culture of doing you and keeping to yourself prevails. That being said, you're liable to give a quick nod, or smile and say, "Hey," if you make eye contact with a passerby. It's common courtesy.

I get that some people are reserved, or simply don't want to engage with others some days. But human to human, if you look into the windows of my soul and look away as I smile, we might as well square up on sight. You got some nerve disrespecting me like that. At the very least, I'll turn and mutter a curse at you under my breath before walking off.

Clearly I'm sensitive about this. Yes, I've grown comfortable buzzing past hundreds of strangers daily without saying anything. But are we so isolated that we can't acknowledge fellow persons bravely moving through life? Would it kill you to try and flash a smile at the stranger you accidentally locked eyes with? It's annoyances like this that separates people who value how interconnected we all are, and people that can look at a story like Tamir Rice's death and say, "Welp, doesn't have *shit* to do with me."

The greatest perpetrators of this blatant disregard for others are folks who didn't grow up in the inner-city. People that rarely have to interact with those they don't share a mutual friend with. I observed disconnected people like this daily during my time at St. Thomas. Even some Black folk who grew up just a half-hour drive away from my St. Paul stomping grounds were guilty of this. Blank stares in response to a head nod that said something like, "Uhh, I don't know you, bruh." *Nigga that's the point*, I'd say to myself in my head. *I'm trying to bridge the gap here.*

Hurt feelings out of the way, I wasn't going to swing or curse at a stranger for walking past me without a greeting. However, when it happens on a relatively small college campus like St. Thomas, you start asking questions about yourself. Like, if I know you're in my eight o'clock morning class three days a week, but you look at me like you don't know me when I see you on the way to dinner, am I just not worth talking to? Do I just keep it moving? I wanted to make friends, damn it! The regularity with which I was getting blown off was maddening. Doubts of the sort were strongest in my first semester on campus. I felt exposed like a dreadheaded nigga at a Taylor Swift show, yet still invisible. Like, people definitely looked at me, but they didn't want to *see* me.

Not all black and brown students felt so conspicuous on St. Thomas' campus. Visibility equated to status, and some Black students had enough of it to be well-received by the general St. Thomas student body. Athletes and those in student leadership positions (e.g. resident advisors, tour guides) enjoyed a significant boost in prestige. If that wasn't your game, you either had to be cool with such students or know incoming St. Thomas students prior to your freshman year.

But I wasn't just Black, and I wasn't just outside of the perceived in-crowd. I was from the East Side of St. Paul, the first in my family to go to college, and the first in my family born in the United States. I couldn't give you the directions to any suburb aside from nearby Roseville, and I probably didn't know you if you weren't my classmate or my neighbor growing up. I was a foreigner in a field of small-town Midwestern folks, hot-shot suburbanites, and private school kids.

Everyone saw me, but no one wanted to. In every instance of a failed greeting with a St. Thomas student slowly walking toward me, all alone, there was a conscious choice to break the gaze. To pull out the phone. To find the grass more interesting than a fellow student (but how that grass stayed so green, even in the winter, *is* interesting. Wealth, man). I can't even count the number of times those techniques were used on me *after* I stared into the souls of these people with a downward head nod and a smile. It wasn't even "The Nod." Shit was formal! I was trying, y'all.

It didn't matter. It simply didn't matter. My face after these countless failed attempts at connecting with my reluctant college peers usually read of held-back outbursts:

I go here too, bitch! Either look at me and smile, nod, whatever the fuck, OR don't look at me at all.

I'm not an extra in your "Off To College" reality TV drama. We did a small group project last semester! Fuck you.

You know you don't have clout like that, stop playin' with me. I'll get to roastin' ol' purified-in-the-waters-of-Lake-MinneTONKA headass.

As the frustration of those moments dissipated, the disappointment sprouted. I wasn't in the lame-ass business frat, student government, a student club, or a varsity sports team. I didn't need all ten fingers to count the number of kids I knew from the bastions of Minnesota's upper-class high schools like Cretin, Eden Prairie, or Hill Murray. I wasn't familiar with Wisconsin or towns bordering Canada or Iowa, and I wasn't planning to get familiar. It felt like no one at St. Thomas had a frame of reference to make sense of what I was and where I came from.

Realizing that you had to be someone on campus to receive a casual hello or a smile with a head nod was sobering. It was even worse realizing there was no reason for anyone on campus to be checking for me. Who was I in this new world I found myself in? If you asked me then, the answer was no one.

2

BMOC

•••

Enrolling at the University of St. Thomas was a reluctant choice—my only choice after the humbling results of my application process—but I felt ready to apply myself, meet new people, and grow. The pajama pants, the blocky low-end Nike sneakers from Kohl's, and '70s afro said otherwise. Between overestimating myself and being so frugal that I still collected pennies off the ground, I was in for a rude awakening at St. Thomas.

Unlike the crowded hallways of Central High School in the rough social mix of St. Paul's Midway area, you didn't make friends at St. Thomas by saying, "Wuss good?" to someone three times a week. You had to be recognizable. You had to show up to club social events, be on a sports team, get a student leadership position, *something* that said you mattered on campus. And if you didn't, you had to try to look like you mattered. It was much like the adult world. How naïve of me to think St. Thomas students wanted to meet new people just for the sake of meeting new people. Cast our nets wider, learn new perspectives, and other wonderful clichés you might find on an admissions brochure.

I realized that participating in lectures wasn't enough for my peers to acknowledge me outside of the classroom. I also learned that meeting a St. Thomas student while they were drunk almost guaranteed disappointment the next time you saw them and remained unacknowledged. I was quick to blame the preppy White exclusivity the school was known for. However, my defense crumbled in the face of a skinny Somali guy named Muhdi Sharif.

Muhdi was the shit. Anyone worth anything on campus had to know Muhdi. The enthusiasm with which students flocked to him as he lounged on the plaza outside of the shiny new Anderson Student Center (ASC) was baffling. The reign of Muhdi Sharif was one of my greatest questions about the strange world of St. Thomas—along with Ash Wednesday and deciding whether or not artichoke dip was good. My first year in college was Muhdi's last, but Facebook updates assured me his networking success had continued into the corporate world. On top of earning cool corporate trips from 3M and appearing to know everyone in the company, "Swag Thursday" survived into his professional life.

Swag Thursday, the embodiment of Muhdi's charisma, is a movement he started at St. Thomas that even the stiffest of White people bought into. Every Thursday, Muhdi rocked bowties, St. Thomas–purple themed outfits, and conventional formal looks. He took pics with football players, White girls, a good friend of his that played for the Chicago Blackhawks, and university administrators. The juice was his.

Muhdi flooded Facebook timelines weekly. He set the standard for freshness on campus. Whether it was a pic with the school's president, or a timely image of himself in traditional Muslim garb with a slick proud-of-my-culture caption, Swag Thursday was everything cool and confusing about an East African Muslim being the face of a private Catholic university's student body. The St. Thomas community viewed Muhdi as the BMOC—big man on campus—without question. I, too, saw Muhdi as a BMOC—a Black man on campus—and had hella questions.

Swag Thursday, really? Just threw swag in front of a weekday and shit is cool now? It seemed too good to be true according to my ego. I was an admirer as much as I was a critic, bordering on envious. I refused to believe it was that easy to be a Black person who mattered on campus, let alone a Black Muslim.

Father Dease, then school president, could be seen around campus cracking jokes with Muhdi all casual and shit. I didn't get it. If I allowed myself to believe Muhdi's social success wasn't some goofy exception, it meant I'd have to change how I thought about St. Thomas. I couldn't continue to believe the campus had no room for students to challenge racial and religious boundaries. Accepting Muhdi's presence as reality meant there was a real chance to be myself on campus, a hip-hop-loving, afro-rocking, Google-searching Ethiopian-American kid. I was still a skeptic, but Muhdi was a natural hot spring in the middle of the frozen white social tundra of St. Thomas giving me a reason to march on. If a lanky, nappy-headed Somali dude could be loved on this campus, maybe I could one day.

Five years after I first saw him coolin' outside the ASC, I gave Muhdi a phone call. It had been a year since I graduated, and I was in a much more positive place about my past and present. Every time I recalled Muhdi over the years leading up to this phone call, my impression of him got brighter. Seeing him thrive on campus fueled my climb out of the pessimistic place I was as a freshman.

Catching up with him was satisfying, and I finally got to ask him why he thought he was so popular in college. The answer was not, "I grew up in the glorious suburb of Eden Prairie, so I knew how to get around," like I thought it was going to be. His response was almost nothing about race and class, and all about his attitude.

"Smiling is a part of our religion, smiling is a charity, *sunnah*, y'know?" Muhdi told me that kindness and greeting people with intention was key. He took it to the next level when he said smiling was actually a Muslim principle, a sunnah, one of a collection of Muhammad's (PBUH)[1] greatest life teachings. Between Swag Thursday and simply existing on campus, Muhdi was doing interfaith work, improving race relations, and branding himself. It was Muhdi's ability to better a community by being his best self that inspired me to make more out of my time at St. Thomas.

I was also surprised to hear that Muhdi viewed the large presence of his high school classmates at St. Thomas as an obstacle to his growth rather than a boost. I was so thirsty to prove he had the privilege of social capital that I didn't consider how shitty it would actually be to have your late adolescence follow you into college. To have people trail you into adulthood who still talked about that one embarrassing thing you did when you were fifteen years old. People that wouldn't feel the urge to help you grow into something better.

Sure, Muhdi had the chance to extend his high school glory days into college. But instead, he took it upon himself to branch out.

His confidence was levels above mine, but Muhdi was just like me: a colorful kid on a white campus canvas just trying to make the picture look good. It was enlightening to know that someone with a racial and religious background like his found so much opportunity at St. Thomas with a simple perspective shift.

Despite the skepticism, freshman Zander was still inspired. *Perhaps being a brown man on campus doesn't have to be complete shit,* I thought to myself as I walked past Muhdi on the plaza one of the last times before he graduated. My attitude began to shift like a tectonic plate, a slow move, but a big one. It was going to take some time, but I was determined to figure out how to be a BMOC.

3
Scrubby

...

If you asked any of my good friends what it would take for the average White St. Thomas student to think I was worth speaking to, I'm sure a wardrobe upgrade would be top of the list. The criticism was loudest when my friends and I pre-gamed for parties as freshmen.

"You're going out in *that*?" My good friend Matt, who was at the neighboring University of Minnesota, stood dumbfounded in the living room of his on-campus apartment. "I can get you different pants bro, honestly." I assured Matt I was fine as we made our way to the kitchen. More Kraken shots were being poured by his roommate from we-drink-anything-because-winter-is-hell Duluth, Minnesota.

Kraken never entered my body after my first month of college. There are some things in life you just don't have to do, folks. Same goes for Captain Morgan, and garbage vodka like Karkov and Aristocrat.

Matt's concern for my dusty look was logical. It was already hard enough to connect with girls, especially White girls, the overwhelming majority at the U of M and St. Thomas. We weren't White, we weren't athletes, and we were freshmen. Hitting a party in pajama pants was a silent but strong plea to be ignored. Dull forest green with black checkered lines, I paired my raggedy pants with a gray hoodie to complete the rolled-out-of-bed look. The way I presented myself literally stressed people out. I was oblivious, a terribly misguided kid who thought I could be taken seriously just because I was nice and smart.

The first time I truly felt bad about my apathetic style was a Saturday morning walking around St. Thomas, hungover after a night out at the U of M. I sported the go-to gray hoodie, matching the day's drizzling rain and cloudiness. My 'fro was kinda crunchy, and my all-purpose pajama pants were haphazardly tucked into my socks to keep the tattered cuffs from dragging along the wet ground. Yonas, a fellow Habesha boy from St. Paul, walked by. He shot me a perplexed look with slightly raised eyebrows. Yonas then gave a polite, "Yo," attempting to hide his appropriate shock at seeing me, a supposed young adult, leave my bedroom lookin' like a walking ball of lint.

The symptoms of scrubbiness were there, but it wasn't diagnosed until two years later. A sit down with Matt and James Thomas, a transfer student and fellow St. Paulite, became a pivotal moment in my college career. By this time the abominable pajama pants were finally quarantined in my closet for good. However, I still looked like I didn't care. Graphic tees, untrimmed facial hair, no dress shoes, scrubby. If I didn't spend as much time in the books (i.e. Wikipedia) and making my speech more measured and articulate, I'd be a y'all-niggas-hiring? nigga.

Beyond race, beyond class, the attempt at looking "respectable" shows people you're trying to adhere to the same world they are. It makes people comfortable with your presence. You become easier to approach, trustworthy even. Despite the race and class implications present in our idea of what "respectable" is, it still would not have hurt me to try cleaning up my look sooner. Simply throwing a $15 dress shirt over one of my beloved Jimi Hendrix tees would take me from "Suh dude?" to "I did reasonably well in that interview."

But it *was* about race. It *was* about class. The way someone styles oneself shouldn't be the greatest factor in determining social worth, but often it's the first and only consideration. If you're not "in" with people, like many students and professionals of color in the United States, the margin of error is even smaller. I didn't have the social capital to afford not looking fresh.

Everyone who knew me noted the comedic contrast between my character and my wardrobe. Like actual good friends, ones who called you out on shit rather than letting you look like a fool in front of others, James and Matt gave me much-needed advice.

"You write all this creative shit. You're smart and have all these great ideas. But if I saw you and didn't know you, I wouldn't be able to tell any of that about you." James' insight was sharp, but real. It's not that I wasn't shit, it's that I *looked* like I wasn't shit. Worse it appeared as if I knew but didn't care that I appeared that way. If I really wanted to be taken seriously, I had to look like I took myself seriously.

Between Muhdi's social success, getting clowned by my friends, and several bouts of sobering self-realization, I started to pay more attention to how I dressed. Hoodies were swapped for dress shirts. Jeans and respectable khakis replaced cotton sweatpants and old polyester Fila trackpants. I even got a pair of non-athletic shoes, some slick, low-budget gray Oxfords that I rocked with anything business casual or more formal. Afros and all-natural nappyheads acquired through sleep were trimmed down to flattops, and later into brush or bald fades.

This version of Zander won a scholarship at a business concept challenge and went out of state to present his own research. Zander that cared about his appearance got to manage a veteran independent hip-hop artist and take a university-sponsored trip to Atlanta[1] to network with artists from the UK and Canada. This Zander traded liquor, weed, and parties for creating his own website, and learning Portuguese and Japanese in his downtime.

The look wasn't just a look. For all the time I spent soul-searching, researching, and shaking my fist at preppy St. Thomas folk, I was way more concerned with actual growth and change than simply looking like I grew and changed. But what my time at St. Thomas helped me accept was that caring about your look didn't have to be pure vanity. For as much as people flex and stunt with nothing to show for it in life, people also use their outer appearance to embody what they're about. Once I stopped being salty about people ignoring my greetings, White girls not going for non-athlete Black dudes, and being forgotten by someone I met on a drunken Friday, I realized there was way more I could have been doing to present myself as someone worth talking to.

Instead of hating on guys who owned suit coats and went to job fairs, I figured my brown skin could be used advantageously in professional settings if I simply looked nice. My perspective shift made campus a social playground rather than a social prison. A fun, low-stakes place to practice navigating the world as a Black adult rather than a place which trapped my true self. Going to St. Thomas meant I was *in*, meaning I finally had access to the kinds of connections my White peers in high school honors courses already had via their parents. People that mattered, people that could help me matter, the social capital I sought. Businessmen, scholars, and other established professionals that seemed impossible to reach when you and everyone you grew up with didn't know money or college. Networks of people and resources that made some people born into them pretentious, but could change the life of someone like me.

You'd be surprised at the number of shocked reactions I received from White adults when they learned of my enrollment at St. Thomas. The reactions were a mixture of, "How the fuck..." and "Good for you!" The shock always quickly masked with flattery. These reactions were microcosms for the attention my Black peers and I felt on campus daily. As irritating as it was, living under that gaze became a great opportunity to change their perceptions of us. To gain the upper hand by showing White America just how bright and polished a brown man can be while they sorted through the broken pieces of their misconception.

Once my outfits fell in line with my attitude, those chances became easier to seize. A Black guy with a flat-top and dress pants at St. Thomas commanded curious attention from faculty, staff, and other people on campus that mattered. That made *me* matter, something I wouldn't have learned in a place that didn't challenge my self-presentation.

If I wasn't already good at swimming unchartered social waters while being true to myself, St. Thomas made me great at it. It was a four-year boot camp for what any good Black liberal college student would call codeswitching. But I wasn't just learning how to disarm White folks who didn't get me. I was also learning how to be genuinely me. Even in a room of familiar immigrant children and Black Twin Cities kids, confidently being myself was something I didn't learn how to do until I got to college. Between the improved grooming, dressing, and networking, I was finally seeing social success at St. Thomas.

I just wanted to feel comfortable as Zander in a space where I was the exception. I wanted to gain influence in that space while genuinely being me. The balancing act between social gain and authenticity never stops as an American of color, but it's a balance I learned to manage as a college student. It's in those uncomfortable moments that I grew comfortable with myself. It's where "looking the part" became about freshness, not frontin'. The environment forced me to project confidence. St. Thomas forced me to stop looking scrubby.

4

Party Elsewhere

•••

Central, my old high school, was a ten-minute drive from St. Thomas' St. Paul campus. I only knew one person from my high school that followed me there. Close, but so far away. However corny or confusing the White kids of Central might have been, at least they were city folk like me. Their college aspirations, much like mine, were either for a bigger experience at a large state school like the University of Minnesota, or, if small and private was the choice, a name-brand experience. Think Tufts, Bowdoin, NYU— schools that made you feel exclusive for simply applying. St. Thomas was neither of those things, but it had a culture of exclusivity that didn't make sense for a school admitting four of every five applicants located in the middle of the 14th largest metro area in the United States.

The isolated nature of St. Thomas' campus struck me as odd on the way to my first campus visit a month before my first semester. No, I wasn't proactive at all in my college search. Anyway, the drive down Summit Avenue was nothing but tall trees and enormous houses until I hit the intersection of Summit and Cleveland. Out from amongst those trees and lavish residences, a group of glimmering classroom buildings popped out, reflecting sunlight off of their perfectly smoothed, limestoney surfaces. Another half a block down Summit from the intersection and I saw the university's official front door, the Arches. They connected two buildings whose imposing Ivy League-like styling added a sense of tradition to the otherwise contemporary design. It was the conclusion wealthy Summit Avenue deserved, as the next block led straight to the Mississippi River.

St. Thomas was a sort of urban oasis. It was hard to believe this existed fifteen minutes from where I grew up. Neighborhoods along Rice Street were full of dull, tattered houses and apartment complexes. They looked sunken, mopey. Then there was Central High School, my charming alma mater in the middle of St. Paul designed by a prison architect, according to a longtime childhood friend of mine. It was formidable, gray, blocky, and had narrow strips for windows on the outside. The houses in the surrounding neighborhood weren't disgusting, but most of them were almost a century old and desperately needed makeovers. Jimmy Lee, the rec center across the street, was recently spruced up, but didn't do enough to change the area's bleh feel. We the people gave the area character. We were what was interesting. Not the buildings, not the houses, us.

Rolling up to St. Thomas' campus, I was pleasantly surprised. It was the kind of beauty I never thought I'd see in my hometown. But unlike the other side of town I grew up in, the things, not the people, made the world of St. Thomas attractive. I was impressed, but not sold on the campus's appeal.

I understood colleges and universities had to look shiny and polished to compete with each other. In that department, St. Thomas was winning. Brand new buildings, new flat screen monitors everywhere, and a big ass display screen for the football field were only a few of the university's cool accessories. All of it would have been so satisfying if the staff and student body weren't so much like the facilities around them: stiff, sterile, unable to adjust to external difference. Products of the environment, I guess. White students and staff were consistently the greatest examples of this.

See, White people in the city are different. They're still decades behind in their understanding of hip-hop culture and race in America, but at least they acknowledge your existence. They can't get away with ignoring you because they *have* to interact with you. From public school administrators to gyms, Target stores, and gas stations, the Twin Cities—the cities proper, NOT the surrounding metro area—hosts a vibrant mix of Black folk and immigrants from Southeast Asia and East Africa. This racial medley of people is too ingrained in the community to be avoided.

White folks truly within the Cities at least try to keep up the pretense that they don't mind interacting with people of color. Yes, the creeping influence of gentrification is quickly making Twin Cities neighborhoods Whiter—don't get me started on housing segregation. However, the chances of a White person having to engage with a non-native English speaker, a non-Christian, or a regular ol' melanated person in the Cities is still much higher than outside of it. On the contrary, substantial interaction with *anyone* of a different background wasn't an expectation many White folks at St. Thomas had growing up. It made for many uncomfortable social situations. Take introductions, for instance.

Greeting White guys at St. Thomas was robotic. I sometimes tried to dap a White guy up, but often would get a stiff ass handshake that strangled my loose fingers. My fingers would get trapped halfway in the guy's grip at a weird angle as he rigidly shook up and down because that's all he knew how to do. My thumb would be like, *I should try and make this as much of a handshake as possible,* and grip the outside of the guy's hand to ride out the awkwardness. Trying to shake up with some of these guys was like giving Siri a command it didn't know how to respond to. You either went with the gentleman's handshake, or basically tried to shake up with a fence pole.

Generally, White Minnesotan St. Thomas students shared something in their social approach. They weren't mean or antisocial, but they were much quicker to filter out people of different cultural identities in their social lives. Unless you appeared on their social radars as a friend of a friend, you didn't expect White St. Thomas students to go out of their way to get to know you. Their capacity to create relationships with people that weren't already in their network, or simply White and Christian, was limited.

Students of color, including Black students, that grew up in White social circles played this game well. Black kids in White social circles varied in their level of connection to the Black social circles I was a part of. Many tried to keep one foot in and one foot out, remaining cool with my friends and I, but not quite as tight as they were with their White friends. Even with connections to this distant group of Black students, getting into St. Thomas' in-crowd through them was a challenge for me.

My first St. Thomas party was a great example of the difficulty I experienced getting a connection to stick. More than half of the party surrounded the beer pong game in the kitchen, and a straight White couple danced awkwardly to the Top-40 mix that was playing. The remainder of the attendees sipped from their red solo cups and dawdled on their phones.

I met an Asian upperclassman at that party. He knew everyone in the apartment that night, spoke with long "o" sounds, and rocked a classy polo with some boat shoes. He was everything I found annoying about St. Thomas minus the subtle racism, standing next to the door sipping a whiskey and Coke. Despite the inane small talk we struck up, I was just glad to have met someone new at a party. The conversation ended ten minutes later with a firm handshake (one I was ready for) and names being exchanged.

I saw that dude around campus several times the following week. I offered a nod and a smile every time. Blank stares came in return every time. It was worse than a moment where you accidentally greet someone you mistook for someone else because I actually knew this motherfucker. I hadn't built my immunity toward these disappointing moments, so it bothered me the entire week.

College parties in general are not much different from the tale of my first St. Thomas party. Even if you went to wild, crowded house parties, it wasn't necessarily easier to forge lasting connections. I thought it would be easier to make friends at the U of M—a staunchly held belief throughout my freshman year. The appeal was obvious: four times the people, ten times the parties, and zero reason to not try and mingle with people you didn't know. Even if you still had to sift through out-of-touch White folk who couldn't carry a genuine conversation, there were more than enough chances to meet people with an array of identities and have a good time.

Being at the U of M on weekend nights helped me understand what was so trash about my social experience at St. Thomas. At St. Thomas, I felt far outside of the culture. On weekends, students either went back home, threw themselves into the cluster-fucks of select bars near campus, or went to one of a handful of off-campus house parties. A good time equated to hours of beer pong and sloppy drunk fake-deep convos you forgot the next morning. The concepts of meeting new people and dancing seemed foreign to the average St. Thomas partygoer. This didn't appeal to me, someone who only needed a quality selection of hip-hop songs as social lubricant. Even if I did want to go to these parties, I was struggling so hard to connect with new people during the week that I had no leads to the turn-up when the weekend rolled along. Leaving campus on the weekends became a no-brainer.

I went to my fair share of ragers at the U. And even when the straight guy-to-girl ratio left my male friends without girls to talk to, or when folks were just too drunk to engage with, the shit-load of new faces and more integrated parties satisfied me for a bit. Matt's new friends were a motley crew of Black guys and a Cambodian guy from the glorious suburb of Eden Prairie, along with an Indian kid from Duluth. They knew a bunch of White people, but made sure to have friends with a variety of identities. The sheer mass of students, and the occasional D1 hoopers and football play-ers passing by, made the U of M feel expansive. There were always more people to meet, always new shit to do. I wasn't trapped into interacting with people that didn't seem interested in me.

Partying off campus satisfied my freshman urge to wil' out. It was an escape; a social life I didn't have to try so hard to cre-ate unlike the scene on my own campus. I didn't have to question myself about how I fit in at the U, never had to leave my comfort zone in order to have a good time. There were enough spaces for quirky brown-skinned kids like Matt's crew and I to be ourselves.

Partying away from St. Thomas did a lot of good for me. However, I was surprisingly unfulfilled from it. The big campus experience of the U of M was an itch scratched, not a hole filled. I soon found myself lost in the waves of people that simply fol-lowed hype, chasing fun rather than making fun. I grew weary of twenty-minute walks across campus just to see if a kegger was ac-tually poppin'. Matt and I stopped scouring through contacts to find girls we barely knew who could get us into frat parties, just to get bored once we got into one. I wasn't creating my own expe-rience. I didn't even go there! I was seeking the familiar, trying to make my college experience more like my high school experi-ence instead of learning from the difference St. Thomas presented me with.

Much like many of my non-White peers who talked a big game about transferring from St. Thomas to the U of M after their first year, I didn't do it. Not only was the process cumbersome, I realized a college experience that challenged me was a blessing in disguise. It had the potential to be something I crafted, something that I could make my own. The U had a Black presence on campus and a strong network of alumni of color. There was an established niche that black and brown students there could find solace in. But rather than cursing St. Thomas for not having something similar, I started to imagine how dope it would be to create a presence of my own. To be my own spectacle instead of trying to follow one.

The right mix of sociocultural factors were in play for an optimistic Black person to succeed at St. Thomas. My friends and I felt stuck, but in the midst of all the bros, snowbunnies, and guys who shot deer for fun, a path to being *that nigga* at St. Thomas was going to be forged. I didn't see it coming, but a couple of new faces and brave movements during my sophomore year were going to give me new life in my mission to enjoy St. Thomas.

5

Snowbunnies

...

"Nah, you're drunk as fuck."

Kendra and I were alone in the basement at a raucous house party on a frosty March weekend. It was my sophomore year. We hit it off a week prior at a different party, her isolation from the rest of the scene piquing my curiosity. She was from Connecticut, a good minute from Minnesota, and she didn't have to fake being bubbly to seem interesting. *She could be...different*, I thought.

Small talk via text happened throughout the week. I kicked it with her while she worked night access at one of the dorms. She listened to some indie rock shit you'd never see on my playlists, but it was fine. She had gotten out of a relationship a couple of months ago and seemed refreshed by my presence. As far as I could tell, she was feeling me.

Fast-forward to next week's encounter, the raucous house party in question. Upon seeing me, Kendra's first words were peppy but slurred, like they came out swimming in the rum and Coke she downed before I got there. She was touchy, loose, but too loose, done before she even got started. Her head whipped around at every new stimulus: a boy, a drink, laughter, a familiar face. She wanted to chase the fun wherever it went, even if it was a few seconds before she decided it went elsewhere.

Kendra scurried off after our chat, so I kicked it with a few friends for a bit. I then wandered the house and struck up several conversations in the following fifteen minutes. I was interrupted by a scouting report from the homie saying Kendra was walkin' around making out with random dudes.

"Huh…"

"Yeah bro, you gotta get her alone or something."

Unlike guys who slapped the "We're talking" tag on a girl to assert exclusive access to her, I wasn't interested in making juvenile claims for someone I had only spent two sober hours with. I went to the basement to be entertained by a beer pong match while she lived life.

The game ended shortly after I got there, and I lingered with a couple of folks after it. As they left to go upstairs, down came Kendra, and a still moment between us ensued. She looked at me warmly and held eye contact, her erratic bullseye landing on me. I was kinda confused, as I saw both the heart flutters and the vapors of alcohol they were gliding on. She drunkenly rocked forward, we kissed, I looked at her, and delivered the eloquent quote you read at the beginning of this chapter. She thanked me, and went upstairs.

Throughout the night my friends relayed info of her continued flirtatiousness, wondering what went wrong downstairs. I assured them I was at peace. They were disappointed, but accepting. Kendra turned out to be a snowbunny, and I had a chance at securing one of these elusive creatures. A chance many of my friends coveted. But the price, a good chunk of my dignity, was too high.

Defining characteristics of a snowbunny can change depending on who you ask. At the term's broadest, a snowbunny is a plain old straight young White woman. A less prejudiced use of the term came with a nuanced view of how social class intersected with race. When I use the term, it isn't just any White girl that is considered a snowbunny. To me, the term comes with a level of social class, sheltered innocence, and flippancy that bewilders anyone who's had to wash dishes by hand or use the same cellphone for longer than a year.

Snowbunnies were flirty. Snowbunnies frolicked where others simply walked. Snowbunnies appeared naïve in a way someone who's never walked a city street alone at night would seem at first glance: uncontrollably giggling, acting drunker than their nearly-full mixed drink suggests they are. Wide-eyed and interested in every boy they talked to, but only if the boys didn't pay too much attention to them. Because much like actual bunnies, they scurry away and make you look foolish the minute you go chasing the shaky little tail. Many of these traits can be applied to women of any racial identity. However, the particular implications of Black men interacting with White women cannot be ignored.

The history of the Black man/White woman dynamic in the United States is everything gross about the games we play for status in this country. Too often we see the Black man and the White woman put one another on a pedestal in their fantasies, then viciously drag each other when things go wrong. The belief that a

Black man can "upgrade" by acquiring a White woman is steeped in colorist misogyny. Viewing a White woman dating a Black man as rebellious is steeped in racism. But who is the victim in this dynamic? Is the woman being preyed upon, or is the Black person being vilified? Black men and White women can be as innocent to each other as Emmett Till and Nicole Brown Simpson. They can also be as threatening to each other as O.J. Simpson and Carolyn Bryant.

Chill out, I know shit escalates when Emmett Till and O.J get brought up. Rest assured, my dating experience at St. Thomas was comedic, not dangerous. But I can't throw race out of the window when talking about it. On the Bogardus social distance scale— a seven-point scale measuring a person's comfort with other social groups (e.g. racial, religious)—the highest level of closeness in social contact is marriage with someone of another social group. Casual sex isn't marriage, but who you physically let in or get into is someone you're getting close to. Your labels mattered in these cases, and "BLACK" was a loud label to wear at a St. Thomas social event.

Given that brief sociology lesson, it isn't hard to imagine why my Black male friends and I attributed some of our failures at mingling with White St. Thomas women to their race. Kendra, with her East Coast, somewhat urban appearance, got me to believe she wasn't skittish in the way I perceived other straight White women at St. Thomas to be. Perhaps it wasn't fair to attribute her actions that night to her Whiteness. She was, after all, recovering from a break-up. She was allowed to make mistakes and get to work through her emotions like any other young adult was. But in the tundra of Minnesota, young Black folk have no choice but to consider Whiteness in every interaction with a White person. And intimacy, even the sloppy, ill-defined relationships that college students tend to get into, was *definitely* thought of in terms of race.

Game-playing mischief wasn't the whole truth of the experience my friends and I had with White women at St. Thomas. However, it was a narrative we leaned on to preserve our fragile man-boy egos and fill the gaps in our shared view of St. Thomas' social life. It made our experience mythical. Night drives became quests, and post-party recaps became folklore. The thrill of the chase, simply trying to find girls that didn't need us to be foreign or on a sports team to talk to us, always made up for the failures.

I wasn't the first nor the last Black guy to get curved by a White girl. The messiness of college party culture added to the frequency of guys missing their shots. As I strolled into parties with a hoodie and some sweatpants on, nonchalant but vigilant, the rest of the observable male species would be clutching to bottles and cups as if alcohol became illegal to drink after college. Girls would dance on each other or cling to their group of friends to lessen the risk of being hemmed in by multiple guys at once, something that looked as unnerving as it sounded. I soon found out it was tough to use the word 'respectable' before 'hook-up', and I watched many of my friends toss the first word out the window in pursuit of the second. The notorious snowbunnies tended to be their targets.

The fall of sophomore year was liberating. My friends and I were nearing our twenties or freshly into them, the feeling of do-what-the-fuck-I-want adulthood was at its highest, and our actual adult responsibilities were at their lowest. This allowed our weekly social experiments with St. Thomas' nightlife to be the most important part of our lives. For all the failures we had with drinking, interacting with girls, or finding parties with good music, it was the stories of failure that ended up being the most memorable. This was especially true in the case of Darrell and his pursuit of White women.

Darrell Macklemore was a trip and a half. Hailing from inner-city Omaha, Darrell was a Black intellectual astute in matters of race relations and social class. He grew up in a place where people across the race and class spectrum were always in close proximity, much like St. Paul. Wading in such a diverse pool of women, interracial dating was a no-brainer for Darrell. He considered himself particularly well-versed in connecting with White women of all backgrounds. He was a "bunny whisperer," his words, not mine. It was this hilarious level of pride that made his hookup failures at St. Thomas exceptionally funny. He never seemed to adjust his expectations. The White girls he went after at St. Thomas came from lofty, isolated class backgrounds that were foreign to him. Darrell never thought he'd have to work his way into an in-crowd in order to be more memorable to a girl.

As he helped me recall four years after leaving St. Thomas, getting a girl's number on Friday or Saturday regularly ended in disappointment for him on Monday. A typical Darrell story went like this: he and some White girl were still buzzed from a party. They left together and flirted with each other the whole ride/walk back. She would spit real game, hands all on him, and ask him about linking up another day. He got her number, maybe made out with her, whatever. A couple of texts go without response, and when he sees her in person days later, she walks by like they never met.

The recollection of these events came fondly to Darrell as he relayed these memories over the phone years later. He can laugh now, but the invisible barriers used to frustrate him to no end.

"These were golden-haired, blue-eyed *bunnies*. Minnesota was like a breeding ground for them outside of, like, Norway...you could play with them, interact with them, but they weren't coming home with you."

Darrell was consistently crushed and baffled. As a self-proclaimed White girl connoisseur, the games some St. Thomas girls played smacked his ego silly. He couldn't understand the light-skinned dudes from nearby private high schools that looked different enough to be intriguing, but were "in" enough to disarm a snowbunny. Darrell's failures at St. Thomas contrasted his hookup successes when partying at the U of M, something he attributed to girls at the U being less wealthy and more approachable. Darrell's experiences on both campuses gave us a glimpse into differences among White women. My hypothesis about the role social class played in a White girl's response to a Black guy's advances gained some steam.

Black girls at St. Thomas who stuck their noses up at Black boys supported my perspective even more. All too often, a pretty daughter of a Black-White couple raised in Minnetonka, Eden Prairie, or similarly affluent suburb would pop up on the scene and give my friends and I hope. As racial politics go, light-skinned girls from outside of the city were the greatest objects of infatuation for Black boys from the city.

"Bougie bitches with no extensions." Better yet, "The light-skinned girls in all the little dresses, good lawd." Kendrick Lamar, from the perspective of his teenaged self, couldn't have been more honest in "The Art of Peer Pressure" about how coveted light-skinned Black and biracial women from the 'burbs are. They stood on the same upper-class pedestal as their White friends, but offered a precious ounce of relatability in the form of melanin. They weren't quite snowbunnies since they stood out from their White peers, but their elusiveness was bunny-like and even more frustrating to working-class Black men thinking their shared skin was an in.

If you identified strongly with your Blackness at St. Thomas, you knew people with shared experience were hard to come by on campus. Seeing other Black people refuse to acknowledge they have anything in common with you really sucked. The phrase "Skinfolk ain't kinfolk" was never more applicable.

Despite the collective lack of game my friends and I possessed, the straight-up disregard of us by some of these Black girls meant more than just another St. Thomas girl treating us that way. The denials had to be firmer, the lack of association clearer. Sometimes it felt like hesitance, like, "If I got to know other Black people here, I'd have to start wondering about my own Blackness." Other times it felt like, "I don't owe them anything. Race doesn't matter, my friends just happen to be who they are. Bye."

Yes, I just assumed the thoughts of people I don't really know. But honestly, am I reaching? Black girls distanced from their

Blackness by class or geography must experience some form of that dilemma when confronted with Black people from a lower class background. The presence of a racial peer with a more "fitting" cultural identity seems to push an upper-class Black or biracial person toward one of two attitudes: associate and become aware of how different they are from other Black people, or dissociate and preserve their status as the standout in their circle of friends.

Though popular, I'm sure those two attitudes are just points on a long spectrum. Light-skinned women across America can vary greatly in how they relate to Black folk with lower-class backgrounds. I mean, compare Zoë Kravitz to Sage Steele, or Zendaya to Stacey Dash. We have to acknowledge racial viewpoints as fluid, otherwise we're just going to trap ourselves in the same boxes we're supposed to be breaking out of. That being said, there had to be some level of an identity crisis happening when guys like Darrell and I walked past the fair brown versions of snowbunnies at St. Thomas.

"Hey, Esther!"

A curly-headed brown-skinned girl looked up from across the atrium of the ASC to see Darrell Macklemore politely wave at her. The stare she served was a cold platter of "What the fuck are you doing?" After an agonizing two seconds, Esther determined she didn't give a fuck about us. She simply looked back down on her phone as if nothing happened.

Darrell, who was determined to prove to me Esther wasn't an uppity sendoff like I thought she was, looked vexed.

"...HA! I thought you knew her bro!"

"I do…we had class together last year. She sat right next to me. We actually spoke often…dang. It's really like that."

Three of my friends went on to develop some level of crush on Esther in our four years at St. Thomas. Along with prominent track and volleyball athletes, the ogling of light-skinned Black suburban girls was as much of a discussion point as trying to appeal to White girls. This never changed, even when my guys upgraded to the bar scene. Different setting, but same people, so same shit.

If we learned anything from this age-old chase, it was the relationship that race had with class. It wasn't just the color of your skin, it was your background. Your associations. Your clout. If you didn't get it from your family or your high school network, you had to find a way to get it on campus quickly. Otherwise, you were just a bystander. Race wasn't the only thing that determined this, but it doesn't take research to know that black and brown men were less likely to have that social capital.

You could talk coin or connects, my friends and I were still broke niggas one way or another. But that's why the allure of the snowbunny never got old. Having one, even for a moment, meant proximity to the kind of aloof freedom a Black kid from the city never had. The kind that true wealth could buy. I didn't want to marry into it, just taste it. Know what overpriced apartments and excessive bar tabs were all about before leaving the bubble of St. Thomas.

Right up until graduation, at least one Black male friend of mine had his sights on a White girl at all times[1]. It wasn't a bad thing, just a reality. If you weren't from the places most St. Thomas students were from, you had to venture across cultural lines all the time. If there were more than a handful of non-White city girls at St. Thomas, this chapter would be half as short. The people I rolled with had to do more to attract people with a smaller margin of error. It was irritating, but it made us focus on creating our own fun before seeking it among others. We began having our own kickbacks and small parties, got new hairstyles, and clowned around in our own circles at other people's parties. We stopped chasing a good time and started attracting it.

Once we accepted the rules of engagement at St. Thomas, we didn't stress 'em nearly as much. These experiences didn't kill our optimism or self-esteem. In fact, they both grew. Parties we once viewed pessimistically became golden opportunities. People we once hesitated to approach became friendly acquaintances. Snowbunnies started hopping over to those of my friends who stopped trying so hard to catch them. Not every night was a win, and not every girl we approached became more than a stranger, but chasing snowbunnies taught us that the rigid barrier of social class can be broken.

6

Sociology

• • •

I spent the last year of my high school career plotting my post-high school greatness. If I was going to UChicago or Duke like I thought I was (my 2.5 GPA told another story), I had to blow niggas' minds. I spent too much time theorizing and studying online debates to not come up with something groundbreaking like "Understanding U.S. Race Relations Through Music Video Comments."

"Sociology is the study of social behavior or society, including its origins, development, organization, networks, and institutions," read the beginning of the dense Wikipedia page for sociology. A couple of minutes later and I was reading about the discipline's biggest names, including Ibn Khaldun and Auguste Comte. While enraptured in discovery, my mom, a firm believer in hard work and good grades, thought I wasn't doing shit. I was turned off from school, and casual Internet surfing didn't seem productive enough to make up for it.

Admittedly, I was useless in high school. But this…this field, these terms and theories, they were going to make me useful. And I knew college taught people these things. All I had to do was graduate from high school and move on. Sociology was going to save me.

I was hooked. Even if most of sociology's prominent faces were old White guys that only worked with other old White guys, they still laid a valuable foundation for understanding today's society. Concepts and principles of human interaction that went beyond place and time, some perfectly suited for our time. My time. A time where race and class weren't perfectly correlated anymore. A time where the social viewpoints of billions of people were accessible to anyone with a wi-fi connection.

Antipositivism—the belief that valid social science research should not follow the scientific method—made me believe I really could preach the gospel about race and class by presenting my comedic journeys through social media, school, and various hoods as data. My discovery of sociology made reading tweets, watching fights, and observing people as I walked the streets of St. Paul feel important.

Second only to rappers, sociologists became important truth-seeking figures in my life. W.E.B. Dubois helped me understand my confusing experiences with race and made me more comfortable being Black in America. Durkheim's concepts of collective consciousness and social facts (i.e. beliefs, laws, values) helped me understand the default views people had about...well, anything. Food, intelligence, love, you name it. I started to understand that clashes with my friends, teachers, and parents about what success looked like was due to a different level of acceptance or rejection of America's social facts. My dreams and interests couldn't exist in their realities. Sociology made this fact concrete. Sociology made it powerful. I could dress my thoughts in terms approved by world-class scholars. I could write unwritten truths. I could finally be respected for talking my shit.

The first college course to take me further into the discipline was Sociology 101 taught by Dr. Pam Banneker. A veteran sociologist in her early sixties, Dr. Banneker was quirky in the way of a White woman who was loudly and proudly down with diversity. She embraced her Southern Christian background, but spoke about pornography with forced frequency to convince us she was socially liberal. She wouldn't hesitate to talk race and ethnicity, but leaned too heavily on students of color to carry those conversations. I applauded her willingness to open those conversations, but asking our Egyptian classmate, "How is it in Egypt?" whenever we learned a new concept became cringeworthy. So was the overzealousness with which she'd rush to me or another Black student for a racial spin on things like conflict theory.

Despite some awkwardness, Dr. Banneker made up for it with a jolly disposition and good discussion topics. I brushed my concerns about her aside to make room for my inflated ego when I was in her class. I quickly realized she coveted my input during lectures. Rather than complain about being gawked at by disengaged White students, I used the attention to steer conversation toward questions that I wanted to explore.

Diving deep into topics was fun because it exposed people who weren't really following along. My White peers weren't slow, but were irritatingly aloof when it came to anything that wasn't of immediate relevance to them. On top of that, no one was ready to do much in a 101 course. I'd be chillin' too if I didn't feel like I had something to prove to myself after a lackluster high school career. Every lecture was an obstacle course I was determined to conquer.

Professors like Dr. Banneker loved this. It brought her joy to have a student who passionately argued that mechanical solidarity was better for a society than organic solidarity. I might sound like a cocky son of a bitch, but please, bear with me. I'm not sure you understand the significance of what I was doing.

I couldn't tell you how many times my Black peers in grade school referred to any kind of academic achievement as "White people shit." Niggas got made fun of for taking honors courses in high school and attending all their classes in a day, let alone a week or a semester. Not caring about school was a point of pride for kids who never saw a family member go to college. Engagement in school meant trying to be something you weren't supposed to be: educated, intelligent, a model of success.

The people I shared apartment buildings and bus rides with decided early in their lives that the classroom was not a place for them. And even if it seemed like they were okay with that, I knew they weren't. So, when I received blank stares from Sociology 101 students while going back and forth with Dr. Banneker about the theory of anomie, I reveled in it. I couldn't get enough. It was refreshing to feel this confident on campus, even if it was only one hour of the day three days a week. I was owning a space that used to intimidate me, and continues to intimidate bright brown kids with working class parents in the same public schools I passed through.

I was doing it for Abeye, the goofy Ethiopian kid with a buzz cut sitting next to me in Dr. Banneker's class. I was doing it for my old neighbor Donny who was still wandering around the block with nothing to do, periodically updating his falsified profile on Facebook. Learning sociology inspired me to continue my education and gave me confidence in the value of my thoughts, qualities I wanted to instill in kids like me one day.

Class was great, but I wanted to stop talking about theories and start using them. So, when Dr. Banneker asked me if I was interested in conducting my own research, I eagerly spewed my vision. And when I got a surprise email from a certain Miss Vivian Jones encouraging me to apply to her graduate school prep program called *Strive!*, I jumped all over it. By the time next fall rolled around, I had presented and published independent research.

I was proud. *Strive!* was the most laborious eight weeks of my life at the time, more tiring than my summer gig at the trucking company my dad worked at. The exhaustion of that job was different from research, however. In the garages, my mind was trapped. I swept, tossed scrap metal out, and did it again. And again. It was the perfect environment for boredom to fester in my mind like mold. My gears tried turning during break periods, but they failed around mechanics that preferred to talk shit about their families and jobs, and give crude updates about their sex lives every day.

Strive!, my first taste of true academic research, was nothing like that. It ripped the cobwebs off of my mind and scraped the rust off with steel wool. It threw a bucket of ice water on my face at seven a.m. and made me run miles. It dragged me kicking and screaming to the depths of my intellect and forced me to search for better answers. If I got lost, it was on me to find a way back. Research at this level was a mental boot camp in forming, defending, and breaking down arguments. I embraced the *Strive!* challenge with enthusiasm, a fitting use of my academic hunger.

When it came time to present my research, people actually enjoyed what I had to say. Some people even learned from me. I had a man tell me he didn't know White Scottish and Irish men were marrying Black women as early as 1850 in New York. Others said they never fully considered that White man/Black woman pairings happen less frequently than Black man/White woman couples due to differences in class desirability.

Research gave my perspective authority even though I was saying things that people with backgrounds like mine intuitively knew. A Black woman riding the 21 bus in St. Paul was liable to say something about the hesitance of White men to date Black women, or Black men viewing White women as upgrades, in a casual phone conversation with one of her friends. Her statements would be just as correct as any of my research findings such as, "Interpretation of the interview data through Social Dominance Theory supports the notion that White women and Black men are more likely to date outside of their races than White men and Black women."

I was applauded for writing unwritten truths, for framing commonsense knowledge as high-class knowledge. Yes, the research helped me gain a historical perspective I didn't have on racial identity and interracial dating. But the major takeaway from that summer experience wasn't feeling smarter, it was feeling *validated.* Like oh, total strangers thought what I said was worthwhile. That was the dopest part of it. I put my intuition through the wringer of academia, and it became an achievement. It was highly rewarding, even fun once I got the hang of it.

My social stock rose as a scholar. I felt like what I imagined the beginning of a rapper's come-up feels like. You get some local buzz on a nice project, some old heads co-sign you, and before you know it you're touring the nation. But like Chance the Rapper after *Acid Rap,* I fought to stay independent.

Academia was much like the music industry: fresh, creative talent flocked to big, slow-footed establishments who offered fame and validation in exchange for your intellectual property. Graduate schools preyed upon undergrad scholars like Lyor Cohen[1] preys upon up-and-coming hip-hop artists. Identity politics weighed heavily in school's decisions to pursue and admit students into their grad programs. This was especially true in social sciences and the humanities. James Thomas, an English major, and Briana, a fellow urban intellectual and sociology major, were both completing their *Strive!* summer research a year after I did. You could imagine the waves that James, Briana and I made among faculty considering you could count the number of Black majors in our respective departments on one hand.

It was around the time Briana and I started looking for exposure that sociology faculty started acting a bit funny. Remember the praise and encouragement thrown my way by Dr. Banneker?

The attentiveness to my research interests? Think of it as Jimmy Iovine from Interscope approaching Chief Keef, selling dreams to trap him into a record deal with an institution that didn't care for Keith Cozart, the kid. Just Chief Keef, the sensation. The deal was a favor with strings attached: Keef got exposure and label resources, but had to be polished before Interscope added him to their collection of profitable rap-pop crossover stars. Unsurprisingly, his deal was chewed up and spit out once it was determined his life and musical output was too raw for the typical rap-pop crossover image[2].

I felt like a sensation, one that Dr. Banneker wanted to refine and show off to the greater world of academia. I later learned Dr. Banneker's recommendation of me to Miss Vivian, as she liked to be called, prompted the surprise email that ushered me into the life of a future Ph.D. candidate. It was a favor from my greatest fan at the time, the faculty member who just couldn't get enough of me. I ignored fleeting concerns that her interest in me was disingenuous. But it was only once Dr. Banneker determined that I didn't fit her star sociologist mold that her true intentions for me were revealed.

So there I was, basking in my newfound academic success, when I started getting side-eyed. Shade came to me in terse emails and cold face-to-face conversations. I soon found out that success in academia had a different meaning to more traditional faculty members. In other words, the ones that cared more about their titles than their students.

Professors are not heartless, but note that it takes the better part of two long decades to get a Ph.D. and become tenured faculty. With the constant pressure to publish work and look good for their university just to earn job security, it makes sense that a professor would prioritize their reputation over true student development. Mentorship isn't necessarily their job, after all. Maintaining a rep in academia meant publishing research every year, and receiving executive producer credit on every piece of student content they could. It also meant initiating students into the right networks so they could show them off properly.

Along with learning how to conduct research, *Strive!* introduced me to the sobering politics of higher ed. Getting into grad school was more than just grades, test scores, and research. You needed faculty allies, and doing research with a professor was the best way to gain one. When I was offered the chance to do research for Dr. Banneker a year after my *Strive!* experience, I knew I had to accept it. I couldn't find any summer research opportunities outside of St. Thomas, so she gave me a deal: run analyses on data she collected from a study on social justice classes—data she admitted was already analyzed—and get to present my "findings" at a sociology conference if I wanted. It was busy work in exchange for a decent bullet point on my academic résumé, a good tradeoff at face value. But I wasn't exploring my own interests, nor was I gaining much useful experience.

When the time came to give Banneker an update by the end of the summer, I told her I didn't want to pursue the project since there were no significant findings of my own. I thanked her for the opportunity and politely declined the offer. Zander, the person, didn't think it was right for Zander, the scholar. Apparently, this was a baffling response. In Dr. Banneker's mind, she threw me a bone with this research project. Zander, the scholar, was being done a pretty big favor if you asked her. The *least* he could do was register for this poster session at the Midwest Sociological Society conference. I then realized that all the times she mentioned that particular conference as a destination for me were her not-so-subtle hints that, "Present if you want," meant, "I expect you to present this."

To Dr. Banneker, that was student development. Plenty of students did the same before me in her time as a professor. Why didn't I just roll with it? Frankly, I wasn't about that shit. The principle wasn't new. Playing bitch to higher-ups as part of initiation was par for the course in Greek life, corporate internships, and sports teams. Professors and students didn't view higher ed like that, but all it took was a step back and an assessment of who held the cards to understand the dynamic. In my case, a Black student trying to appeal to a White professor in a *social sciences* program, you had to be blind to miss the politics.

I tried to play the game the following semester. I was transparent in letting Banneker know of other commitments, but assured her I could easily finish the poster before the conference. While the establishment of a Black student club on campus and the completion of my major coursework felt like big steps toward my personal development, I saw the value in going to that conference. I told her I could finish a presentable poster ahead of her proposed schedule, despite a minor pushback on one of the checkpoints.

Banneker, on the other hand, was furious that I was doing anything other than her research. After an initial email of "ok," she sent another email minutes later saying, "I've given this some more thought. The semester doesn't get any easier...We are done with this."

Shortly after Banneker's hasty cancellation of our partnership, Miss Vivian hit me with an email expressing her disappointment in me. Turns out Dr. Banneker went straight to Miss Vivian in a fit of frustration about my foolish priorities and how difficult I was to work with. *Petty*, I thought while I read the email. I guess there was little value in building a community for underserved students, or focusing on my classes. Apparently, I was the one being frustrating, the one that wasn't quite "getting it."

Despite the failure of my partnership with Dr. Banneker, I was accepted to present my *Strive!* research at the Spring 2015 McNair Conference at the University of Maryland. I figured this would more than make up for not presenting Dr. Banneker's research. I was broke though, so I needed the Grants and Research Office (GRO), home of the *Strive!* program, as well as the sociology department to support me. Thankfully, the GRO contributed $500 through their traveling grant program. Their protocol also stated they'd add an additional $250 if the student's major department also provided support.

I didn't know how to formally ask for money, but I assumed faculty were familiar with the process. On that assumption, I sent a pretty straightforward email to the Chair of the sociology department requesting her help with funding. I won't bore you with the details, so here's a paraphrased version of the email I sent:

Yo, I got accepted to present at a conference in the spring. I talked to the GRO and they said I gotta come to y'all to get full financial support, so let me know what's up.

Zander

In hindsight, this wasn't the most helpful request. Clearly, emailing is a skill I neglected for a while. I could have explained everything about the conference and the GRO grant that I just explained to you. I could have flattered the Chair[3] and asked politely for her support, thanking the department's faculty for getting me so far in my academic career. But I didn't consider this to be another faux pas in the same vein as not presenting Dr. Banneker's research.

Lo and behold, it *was* another faux pas. What I thought was a clean and concise email was apparently another fuck up. I wouldn't be talking about it in such a serious way if it wasn't treated as such by these particular faculty members. As a heads up, Miss Vivian told me she was contacted by the Chair about my crude email. *Again with the snitching*, I groaned. It felt like I was getting written up for detention in elementary school. These professors that didn't know what to do with me were basically handing me to their Black coworker and saying, "*You* deal with this." Seeing this as a teachable moment, Miss Vivian quietly forwarded me the email from the Chair regarding my funding request.

Apparently the Chair, "would have preferred that Zander sent me a more professional request." Fair. Also, "repeated attempts by several department members to provide some mentoring to help him along in his development have not been successful." After this came a warning that if I, "continued to comport" myself like that, grad school, "would be a bumpy ride." Last but not least, "I have asked Zander to provide the documentation requested and if he follows through (he often does not), I'll see what we can do."

"The fuck?!" Briana was stunned after reading the email. "You was just asking about some funding! Like, we don't know how the shit work. You weren't rude or anything."

"I know...I understand professionalism but 'comport'? They want us looking like soldiers or some shit. Also, 'often does not follow through'?? Got me *entirely* fucked up."

Again, I wasn't "getting it." I was making the wrong people unhappy. That, plus the heavy shade at my supposed lack of integrity, had me hot. Sorry I didn't want to subject myself to a professor's irrelevant-ass research just to get brownie points. Sorry for assuming faculty knew everything about funding conference trips. Was I supposed to apologize? Was I supposed to do research that didn't help me grow just for a letter of recommendation? Fuck, man.

It wasn't that I turned down these "repeated attempts" at mentorship, it's that I turned down these offers bluntly refusing to do whatever they asked just to be considered a real scholar. It's still not lost on me that Dr. Banneker was trying to do me a favor, but I struggled to understand why turning down that favor warranted the kind of criticism that her and the Chair lobbed at me. Maybe the questions should have been, "What does he actually want?" instead of, "Why isn't he playing along?" I see how my behavior could be frustrating to Dr. Banneker and the Chair. But it seemed like their damaged pride in the significance of academia was being taken out on me.

Beyond the battle to figure out what a "good" scholar was, the Chair's email left my pride bruised as well. It made me feel like one of the many Black kids I grew up with being written off by teachers and administrators. All they could ever say was, "We *tried* helping them. We *gave* them chances."

It reminded me of an incident during my elementary school gifted and talented program. Maggie Craig, the head of the program, was supervising us during our activities. She looked out at some Black students messing around in the hallway, skipping class and irking her with the noise they were making while we worked on problem-solving exercises. Some students were annoyed by it, and one asked something to the effect of, "They can get back on the right track soon, can't they?" With a disgusted look of disappointment, Craig responded, "No, it's too late for those kids." They were all twelve years old at most.

Many of the same things were said about Briana during her time as a declared sociology major. A fellow East Sider from St. Paul, Briana also saw much of the same treatment her black and brown peers received throughout her time in the public school system. *Those* students. Students that had better relationships with the detention supervisors than the teachers because their detention supervisors were the only adults that had the patience for students yet to figure themselves out. Otherwise, they were inconveniences. Lost causes before puberty.

Briana didn't hear a word from Dr. Banneker or the Chair when she was accepted to present at a Yale University conference. Likewise, Banneker and the Chair were out of the picture by the time I was working at the entrepreneurship school my senior year. The disappointing part is that my entrepreneurial life is completely based on my experiences with sociology. I feel like Dr. Banneker and the Chair could have appreciated my shift if they tried to understand my interest in sociology beyond churning out research. But where other faculty stopped caring, a certain Dr. Smith went above and beyond.

Dr. Buffy Smith, a tall, peaceful Black woman who never let her hair grow beyond a mini-fro, began serving as my faculty mentor during my *Strive!* research project. From Milwaukee, Wisconsin, a notoriously rough city for Black people, Buffy triumphantly worked her way up as a student to the University of Wisconsin, a perennial top-five grad school for sociology from which she earned her Ph.D. Even as a tenured professor, she insisted her students called her by her first name or "Buff." Noting how personable she was upon meeting her, it came as no surprise that her life's focus was mentorship of at-risk (i.e. low-income and typically not White) college students.

She didn't hold back her passion for mentorship, even in her role as a professor. Buffy took more pride in getting a student to laugh at her corny jokes than she did in teaching eye-opening classes like "Race and Ethnicity" or "Privilege and Power." Buffy cared more about the student than the student's work, which almost always led to better work. Her approach to sociology as a discipline was aligned with the pure understanding I had of it before college: a box of tools that aid you in becoming a better member of society while being true to yourself.

Meeting with Buffy a year after I graduated was enlightening. She was now an associate dean, one who remained every bit the humble mentor figure I remembered. Her memories of me were fond, and she affirmed much of my recollection of who I was as a sociology major. "When you revealed more explicitly that you were going to take your sociology background into entrepreneurship, it wasn't a big surprise. I always thought there wasn't a particular discipline that could define you." She was in tune with me, the person, before she tried to understand me as a scholar. Of the figures in the sociology department that tried to guide me, she was the only one that didn't see me as a disappointment for taking my intuition to another field.

She seemed disheartened when I told her about experiences with other faculty spoiling my view of academia. To my surprise, she shared a similar story. For years I saw Buffy as a revolutionary mind and personality who always planned to stick to the script of an institution. It was funny to hear this sage-like beacon of a woman describe her younger self, an irrepressible spirit naïvely buzzing around with dreams of her research saving the world. *Just like me when I first met her*, I thought. A cute yet sobering realization.

As glad as I am to not be in grad school, I don't think college is evil. But I'm definitely jaded. Higher education is just as much of an industry as any other. The higher you go, the more it becomes about pumping work out at the expense of passion. When you meet people that care more about you than what you can produce for them, you count that blessing. Otherwise, that's life.

Rap game, class game, damn near the same thang. But as a young person trying to leave a mark on the world, you gotta learn how the world works first. It was a privilege to learn industry politics in a protected space like college, but the truths themselves are just as harsh.

7

GRAD School

•••

Miss Vivian was as stern and Black aunty-like as the name Miss Vivian suggests. I got a lotta love for her. She was one of the few staff members at St. Thomas that made personal and institutional investments in Black and first-generation college students. And she was tough, goddamn it. Every conversation with her was a test.

If you were a young Black kid roaming around campus and happened to encounter Miss Vivian, you were not ready. You would never be ready. Her unsolicited advice on advancing in life consisted of two words: "GRAD school." She emphasized that first syllable in the way someone trying to sell you the dream of a faraway magical destination would: "The Wonderful World of DISney!" "HOGwarts!" "GRAD school!" Yep, just like that.

There was nothing wrong with encouraging undergraduate students to pursue more advanced degrees, *especially* students who were the first in their families to get far enough to meet this oh-so-serious woman. What she did for dozens of black and brown students before me was phenomenal, sending them off to Master's and doctorate programs around the nation fully funded by the programs they were attending. Her years in higher ed as a student and a staff member not only exposed her to opportunity, it gave her the ins and outs of graduate school: how to network with professors, sculpt the perfect application, and, most importantly, how to get students paid.

Miss Vivian's presence at St. Thomas was militant. She moved like a rogue government agent planning a coup—in the system not to change it, but to take it over. She was there to *play the game*, a catchphrase of hers that summed up her mindset.

"I was like, 'Damn lady, leave me *alone*. I just got here like last week, I don't even know where all my classes are!'"

Johnny retelling the story of his introduction to Miss Vivian was hysterical. A cool, fast-talking Chicago kid who transferred to St. Thomas from a small school in rural Illinois, Johnny knew how to acclimate himself smoothly. There was nothing smooth about Miss Vivian's heavy-handed approach to selling students on the idea of graduate school.

"Do you know the chair of your major department?"

"...No."

"Do you know what you're doing after you graduate?"

"...Nah."

"What is you *doin'*, baby? You gotta get a start on it!"

Miss Vivian handed Johnny a brochure for her newly branded research scholars program. *I seen this nigga wit the afro here before,* thought Johnny before he knew who I was[1].

"Take a look at this and let me know what you think."

"Aight."

"And make sure to focus on your studies 'cause your bachelor's degree is not enough these days. See, most people, they walk across that stage and say, 'I got this diploma.' But what you got in the other hand? If you don't have something that says, 'I got a plan after this,' you're just gonna be like everyone else you graduated with. You gotta *play the game.*"

"...Aight."

Johnny wasn't ready. Johnny didn't *want* to be ready. Understandably so, most people don't want the life of an aspiring Ph.D. Why bust your ass in college just to compete to get into a harder level of college for at least four more years? And, ideally, you had to do that right out of undergrad. No better way to show commitment to a university's graduate program and warrant full funding than to let them know that I'm-taking-a-break bullshit wasn't an option for you.

And this wasn't like an application to an undergrad school. No no nooo, you couldn't just slap your 3.5+ GPA on a piece of paper with a good test score and count down the days until your acceptance letter pops up in the mail. You had to have a portfolio. A curriculum vitae. *Work*, fam. Lists of research, poster presentations, paper presentations, who your faculty advisors were. Did they have Ph.D.s? No? Ha! Get new ones.

Not to mention you have to customize your personal statements for every school you apply to. This means more research. Which schools are you interested in? Do you want to do a sociology program? Social psychology? Which faculty members do you want to pair up with during your time there? What are their research interests? Do they align with yours? What *are* your interests, by the way? Have you figured that out yet? Keep up. The GRE is coming up; this is the summer heading into senior year. You been studying? Do you know what verbal score you need to be competitive? You gon' get it, right? Huh?!

Sharp inhale, long exhale

Aspiring to be in a graduate school program of any sort is valiant. But if you took it even half as seriously as Miss Vivian and her research scholar program students, it looked crazy.

My belief in the value of graduate school was strong the summer after my freshman year. Dr. Banneker's praise set me up for Miss Vivian's strong sell of *Strive!* via email several weeks before the end of my first year at St. Thomas. They both had me convinced in my worth as a scholar. I believed there was no better way to change the world with my ideas than to become a full-blown academic.

I soon found out that intelligence and curiosity were only prerequisites to the lifestyle of an aspiring doctoral student. *Strive!* was about more than just cultivating your research interests. It was about being molded into the look and feel of a Ph.D. candidate. The cohort structure was meant to reflect cohorts in graduate programs across the country. The hefty reading and writing assignments were not terrible on their own, but soon became stressful on top of the work we were doing for our own research. There was always a deadline, always hours of typing to do, a constant grind meant to test you.

We were taking cohort pictures the summer heading into my sophomore year, around the beginning of the annual *Strive!* Research Scholars summer program. The cohort consisted of four intelligent, mild-mannered, mature female students...and me. Conventional poses, forced smiles, and business-casual attire created the mood for the occasion. All things I had little patience for.

Walking out of that session, Miss Vivian ragged on me for how difficult I could be during some of the simplest processes.

"Honestly, Miss Vivian, I just have a hard time conforming."

"Well Z, you're gonna have to if you want to be a scholar."

That moment was the beginning of the end, but I didn't know it at the time. The breakup process, whether with a person or a way of life, tends to start long before the official end. An event you thought was inconspicuous slowly turns out to be a clear first sign of a disconnect in hindsight. My first conversation with Miss Vivian about conformity was such an event. What I thought was a negligible remark about taking photos was actually the core of my dissonance with Miss Vivian: what it meant to be a model scholar. She had a formula long before I even knew what graduate school was, and *Strive!* was just the start of her unsuccessful attempts to plug me into that formula.

Strive! was created when St. Thomas, like many of the schools that had the illustrious McNair Scholars Program, lost federal funding to keep the McNair program. *Strive!* served the same purpose as McNair: to provide resources for high-achieving first-generation college students and students of color to conduct independent research and prepare for success in graduate school.

Miss Vivian ran McNair during its final years at St. Thomas and spearheaded the *Strive!* movement. Any student *Strive!* recruited was a student she recruited. Any student that got into a graduate school fully funded through *Strive!* was a student *she* got into graduate school fully funded. Likewise, any student that came through *Strive!* and did not meet the strict expectations of the program was a student that personally failed her. Students who did not complete the *Strive!* program or prematurely quit the grad school path were on Miss Vivian's shit list, and they knew it. She didn't hold back disappointment, and she didn't hesitate to use stories of disappointing students to motivate her current ones.

Despite Miss Vivian's less-than-pleasing response about selling your soul to academia, the life of a scholar hadn't fazed me yet. I was doing too well. It still felt like the right path to turn my perspective into money, power, and respect. But getting real respect in academia was hard. I soon found out positions of power were extremely hard to attain and required a lot of grunt work and sucking up. And money? Pfft. Let's just say most faculty don't think their students are gonna become anything like Marc Lamont Hill or Cornel West. To get to the point where you could even *think* to make a living off of what you had to say, it took most people a decade of research, teaching, and publishing.

By sophomore year, the sharp criticisms in Miss Vivian's emails had become a regular part of life. Along with reminders to my cohort to prepare for a mandatory spring semester poster presentation, Miss Vivian checked on our academic progress weekly. There were always programs to apply for, conferences to look at, and professors to connect with. Feedback would go from, "Unacceptable!" and something to the effect of, "Are you sure grad school is a priority?" to "Outstanding work!" in the next email. My *Strive!* peers were no stranger to the persistent good cop/bad cop tactic Miss Vivian employed, but we never fully got used to her intensity.

Looking back, her approach was effective. It's hard to get a bunch of bubbly college students to give full professional effort on research when classes, extracurriculars, and a social life were constant distractions. An admissions counselor would see those activities as signs of a complete, balanced college experience. Miss Vivian saw them as obstacles to a student's most scholarly self. Despite her good intentions to keep us on track, her suggested way of life as a scholar simply wasn't right for most college students. Even people that willingly went down this rigorous path knew it was overbearing at times.

My dissonant relationship with the sociology department and the never-ending demand of grad school prep were weighing on me. I began to realize that the students Miss Vivian branded as disappointments were not bad scholars, they just decided they had enough of this lifestyle earlier than most people on the journey. She spoke of students that didn't go to graduate school, or even those that did Master's programs rather than doctorate programs, as if they got away from her. As if they broke her heart or something. For as much as Miss Vivian did to teach us the ropes of grad school, her one-track understanding of success definitely had a dark side.

As I mentioned earlier, her commitment to getting people into doctorate programs made her look down on pretty much everything else that could be seen as developmental: My time at student clubs? Cute. Good grades in a semester? Cool, but did you get into a summer research program yet? Starting a blog? Boy, the only publication that *really* matters is research.

Buying into Miss Vivian's approach meant seeing grad school as the only way to be your best self. The goal was to be a complete scholar, not a complete person. More than anything, "complete" meant completely focused on *the game.* Miss Vivian's ideal scholar treated every minute on a college campus as a chance to impress a graduate school recruiter. The type of student who did an independent study instead of a fun class for elective credit. A student who went to a professor's office hours despite having an "A" grade. Someone who was always filling out some kind of application, whether it was a research program, scholarship, grant, conference, anything to prove their commitment to academia.

I was passionate about racial identity and its intersection with social class. But as much fun as I had exploring these topics, the constant grind of research dampened the joy. So when James Thomas told me he was an Entrepreneurship major, it was a needle of light hitting me in the eye. I had no idea there was an entire school on St. Thomas' Minneapolis campus dedicated to that shit. They even had the Fowler Business Concept Challenge, a call for students of all majors to take a chance pitching a business idea and winning a scholarship as large as $10,000. It was a chance James Thomas presented as worth taking, so we both seized it.

James and I were still about this grad school life, but damn. We wanted to know if our ideas could be taken seriously off the bat.

We wanted to know our ideas had value beyond the classroom. We wanted to have an impact *now*. Outside of his studies, James was always raving about new business ventures and money-making schemes. Between his half-baked ideas, best-seller book wisdom, and quotes from motivational speaker Eric Thomas, James could be a little obnoxious. But the hunger was real. We shared an entrepreneurial spirit, and had deep mutual interest in pop culture, media, and how people consumed those things. It was this interest that drove our respective research projects.

Research through *Strive!* gave James and I historical perspective, and sharper tools to dig into our topics of choice. But the Fowler Challenge reignited our passion, giving us a chance to come up with solutions to issues we felt strongly about. Between smoking sessions and chats while hoopin', we soon had a proposal put together for a website dedicated to engaged pop culture consumers. We called it Slightly Sophisticated Entertainment, a place to host the madness of trendy news, music, and other parts of pop culture in a community that encouraged thoughtful and inclusive interaction.

Our proposal made it to the semifinals, where we were given the chance to present. A White judge called the idea an educational World Star, a surprisingly apt comparison. It was dope. The judges and facilitators of the contest understood the vision James and I had. They understood *us*: our passions, our backgrounds, the value of our perspectives. The judges thought our idea could actually impact people. They thought it could be brought to life. Meanwhile, research wasn't giving us tangible next steps aside from, "Do more research." I understood that a body of work can be compiled as a scholar over time, but the Fowler challenge made me feel like there was a better way of doing so. One where we didn't have to *play the game* to be respected.

Despite our reluctance to *play the game*, James and I were still playing it well. Even in the midst of our excitement during the business concept challenge, James and I were focused on adding to our résumés for graduate school applications. We were fortunate enough to both get accepted to present research at the University of Maryland's Spring 2015 McNair conference. It was an honor, and a huge step forward as scholars. With Miss Vivian impressed and a trip to the East Coast lined up, everything was going right for us. Well, at least until James missed his flight (headass), so it was just me representing the university at this conference.

The conference hosted a grad school fair. Recruiters from graduate schools across the nation flocked to connect with all these bright young students of color. One recruiter in particular was a Master's student studying statistics at Cornell. She took a liking to me and we discussed my research interests. In my desire to channel entrepreneurship into my research, I added a piece to the website concept James and I pitched in the Fall. *If the site could get consistent visitors*, I thought, *I could use their posts as qualitative data for research. I could still build the site while getting a Ph.D.!*

The graduate student from Cornell thought it was brilliant. As far as research methods go, it was unconventional. But she assured me that some schools would find it refreshing and valuable. The feedback made me hopeful. Maybe grad school wasn't so stiff after all. Building the website could be a foundation for my creative endeavors and a tool to help me pursue the highest of education.

My newborn optimism followed me home, all the way into the next meeting I had with Vivian. It then died under the spirit-crushing weight of that conversation. I felt like Will in *The Fresh Prince of Bel Air* whenever Uncle Phil squashed one of his hare-brained ideas.

Miss Vivian didn't even try to entertain me. "Listen Z," she said with a firm, measured tone, warning me of the incoming let-down. "You can't get into a program and take what you want from it. You have to be *fully committed.* This business stuff can't be done with your scholarship. You have to choose one and stick to it."

Maybe I was reaching. Perhaps the Cornell recruiter from the UMD conference gave me bad advice. Maybe it's just 'cause I'm a Sagittarius and we're archers aiming at too many targets for our own good. Maybe I'm writing this book to regain some of the scholarly clout I left on the table. But once Miss Vivian told me I had to choose between pursuing a passion project and spending another four years in school proving my ideas are worth something, the decision was made.

I went my entire senior year without communicating with Miss Vivian. Earlier, she had kicked out five of the seven students from the 2014 *Strive!* cohort for failing to complete their spring poster presentation. Many of my friends were in that cohort, and their bitter end with the *Strive!* program fueled my desire to distance myself from Miss Vivian. For a year, I started seeing Vivian's approach as selfish. Self-righteous guidance from an old head that did more harm than good in today's world. The only thing that put an end to my vilification of Miss Vivian was a chance encounter outside of the student center several days before I graduated.

It was May. The campus was in full bloom, and Vivian's dress was similarly bright and floral. She asked me how I was and I reciprocated, both of us squinting and shielding our faces from the strong yet welcomed sunshine. I told her I was running the website I pitched in the business concept challenge a couple of years back. She said she was proud and glad that I was "doing *something*." I'm not sure if she did or will ever buy into my alternative route toward truth-finding, but she seemed to have respect for my decision. We wished each other well and parted.

I did not go to grad school right after graduating from St. Thomas. I don't plan on going to grad school any time soon, if at all. If a student told me they were in the *Strive!* program, I'd be more likely to say, "Yo, be careful," than "That's awesome!" But I respect Miss Vivian for what she does, and I'm grateful she put me through her program. Dissecting a text, writing clearly, and forming your own arguments are skills that many college students take for granted. Skills that have gone a long way for me personally and professionally. I don't think dragging people kicking and screaming into a program like *Strive!* is the best way to get students of color to figure this out, but it's a great option for a lot of students.

I've always appreciated Vivian's commitment to teaching these skills and making that path a reality for many. That being said, you don't have to go through any of that if you don't want to. At the very least, don't let the dream of life-changing research blind you to the fact that academia operates much like any other industry—politics, superficial commitments to diversity, all that good stuff. So unless your desired profession requires a doctorate degree, bump that. Get this money. Go make a website, write a book, do you. It's 2017, brand yourself! Don't rely on a university to give your ideas a platform when you can do it on your own.

8

The African Apartments

•••

Though the campus climate left much to be desired for students of color raised in the States, St. Thomas' community of international students was super live.

Spanning five continents and countless cultural backgrounds, the international students lived their American lives to the fullest. They were vibrant and easy to get along with. There were Saudi Arabian dudes who looked like they flew straight from the King's palace to come to school, draped in traditional garb and classy designer wear. Chinese and Indian students showed up in droves on campus. Various South Americans—Brazilians, Colombians, and Venezuelans—and Eastern Europeans also featured heavily in this mix of students. Miscellaneous additions like an Ethiopian-Italian boy and an Egyptian student or two rounded out the international community.

Several students from this blender of internationals ended up becoming prominent members of the St. Thomas community, like ambassadors or representatives of all things non-American. Come to think of it, every non-White subgroup within the student body had a couple of trusted reps that interacted with others on behalf of their people. Like diplomats, except, what the fuck? We all went to the same school. It felt like St. Thomas couldn't recognize more than a handful of bright young students that weren't White. Regardless, the international students definitely had a presence.

As much as I messed with the Zizos, Gauthams, and Diegos of the world, the African internationals *truly* had it poppin'. Many were Ugandan, sprinkled with men and women from other nations like Congo and Ghana, creating a lively potpourri of African students. Along with the occasional Middle Eastern and South Asian (i.e. Indian and Bangladeshi) tenants, the African internationals lived in two school-owned apartment buildings some of my friends affectionately called the African Apartments.

Despite being right across the street from the student center, the African Apartments were a world away from the bland undergrad campus atmosphere. The site of some of my harshest FIFA lessons. The site of my first time smoking hookah. Also where I first tried hookah with weed (mmm...). A place where my identity as a first-generation African-American was seen in a raw but gentle perspective. A place where I could feel comfortable treating acquaintances like family, taking food and drink without having to ask or feel indebted to some stingy-ass upper-middle class White boy[1].

It was like being at my aunt's or back home with my parents during *buna* (coffee) time. Reciprocity always worked itself out because everyone had love for how they were being treated by others. We all shared, we all received, we all waltzed into people's apartments without knocking. It was therapeutic for me, a place where people meant what they said, a place where a brown-skinned person didn't have to be defensive or explain themselves. It was also the residence of my greatest entrepreneurial partner-in-crime.

At about 5'7", Hughbert and I stood eye to eye. He was a comfortable balance between stocky and portly, and was often seen rocking fitted caps, solid-colored polos and hoodies. I knew him from the various events he worked as a videographer for St. Thomas' yearbook. He was lowkey, but easy to find if you were looking for him.

The summer before junior year was transitional. My love for soccer sprouted during long days watching that year's enthralling World Cup. I discovered my inherent disagreement with the industry they called academia. I also wanted to start getting my truth out in creative ways. Realizing the hoops I had to jump to be considered a credible scholar, I started thinking of other ways to get my ideas out.

Instead of thirty-page papers full of sociological jargon, I began writing verses daily. Spoken word, poetry, rap, whatever. I also started writing comedy sketches detailing my life in college, kinda like the six young Black men on the YouTube channel Dormtainment. Between YouTubers like them and DeshawnRaw, I had all the proof I needed to say Black male social perspectives translated into great media content. To get my start behind the camera, I enlisted Hughbert to help shoot and edit a video idea I had.

My career as a sketch artist stopped as soon as it started, but it was only the beginning of the partnership between Hughbert and I. The real appeal to Hughbert's ability wasn't the camera work. It was his ability to make something as complex as Adobe Illustrator simple for someone like me who didn't know anything about the software. I had seen him work on projects in a lab on campus before. He made technical mastery seem attainable. To him, learning a skill was simple: try different things until it worked.

A computer science major in a joint Bachelor's and Master's degree program, Hughbert was a true tech nerd. Experience was his favorite teacher, so he threw himself into projects and only stopped to revise or look something up when he encountered an obstacle. More impressive than the tips and tricks he had up his sleeve was how quickly he could teach them. The surprises got better once we started hanging in his own element.

It didn't take long for Hughbert and I to forge a friendship. I started to frequent the African Apartments soon after. Philipo, a fun-loving Tanzanian-American one year my senior, was the first to formally introduce me to the tight-knit community. Philipo and I rolled through on weekend nights, hours before the rowdy residents of the apartments left to take the party downtown. The pregame festivities were my highlights at the apartments for a while since my twenty-first birthday was more than a year off.

Heineken was the foundation for a night of drinking, the official mainstream beer of sub-Saharan Africa. Various bottles of hard liquor were spread on the glass table in Guelord's living room. A tall, gravel-voiced Congolese guy, Guelord was the fraternal twin to the equally tall, much goofier Gauthier. Where Guelord would give me shit in between talking to his fellow French-speaking Africans, Gauthier would joke and make small talk about classes and other weekly routines.

With my newfound interest in FIFA, the twin brothers, along with Philipo, enjoyed the chances they had to school me. Gauthier marketed his FIFA skills as "Equal-opportunity ass-whoop" when he'd tag us in Facebook posts. I don't get scrubbed often these days, but I've come a long way from Friday night FIFA 15 defeats.

When it was warm out, we congregated in the space between the two apartment buildings. A wooden park table with benches on each side was set up on a flat, sizeable concrete square surrounded by grass. People entered the mini-courtyard either from the side facing the street, or the side connected to the alley behind the two apartment buildings. Foldout chairs were sprawled, music came out of someone's car or speaker system, and one of several Ugandan guys would rotate as grill masters, firing up some chicken on occasion. *These guys are dope*, I'd think to myself. *They're literally doing the same shit they'd be doing back home.*

My newfound network of friends enhanced my experience at St. Thomas greatly. As an Ethiopian-American, the culture of the African Apartments was familiar enough for me to interact with, but distant enough to require genuine work to understand. We swapped music tastes and perspectives on current events, borrowing each other's lenses to see the world differently. Newer hip-hop artists were as intriguing to my foreign friends as their medley of Ugandan pop, Afrobeats, and dancehall was to me. I helped them understand Blackness in America, and they gave me an honest and friendly look at the spectrum of meanings African and American had.

The tenants of the African Apartments helped me accept my cultural background at a time where that was difficult. My Ethiopianness mingled awkwardly with my Americanness, but being around other Africans trying to figure out race and class in America was comforting. They were serial optimists, always believing the best was on the horizon. And most importantly, being around them in their element was fun. Too wrapped up in drinking, dancing, and exploring my African identity, I didn't ever think the start of Zander the Entrepreneur would be there.

Soon after our attempts at making videos that summer, Hughbert sucked me into the world of online money-making. I was already impressed with his ability to make quality low-budget videos. But "tips and tricks" weren't good enough terms to describe the magic Hughbert had when it came to the Internet in general. Hughbert understood the ins and outs of creating online content, finding and using tools to make it, market it, and get paid for it. Ever wondered how online ads worked? How websites get built? How certain things pop up on Google above others? One conversation with Hughbert about the Internet was like learning the magician's secrets. Every other sentence was another eye-opening fact.

Over the next year, Hughbert revealed to me his extensive entrepreneurial résumé. He showed me a blog that created automated posts and generated thousands of dollars in revenue in its prime. He showed me places where you could get industry standard business products like logos, business cards, and video voiceovers for less than $10. He showed me a site he made that provided summaries of the daily 106 and Park Top-10 lists back when the show was active on BET. He manipulated the keyword SEO (online visibility) so well that his site used to show up on a Google search of "106 and Park" before the show's actual BET page did.

Underlying his online money-making was the fact that he was a self-taught web developer. He learned HTML, CSS, and JavaScript through YouTube, Stack Overflow, and other sources of coding knowledge between his time in Uganda and the U.S. Meanwhile, some Americans I knew still hit "Reply All" to mass emails.

Hughbert's one-man tech academy invoked stories of child engineering prodigies from various African nations. You know, the special ones that generate electricity for the whole village and shit. They're well-intentioned stories, but those kids are framed as one-of-a-kind diamonds in the rough. Anyone who spent a day seeing Hughbert's work and the intelligence displayed by his neighbors, many of them fellow computer science majors, would be convinced this was happening daily in Kampala, or Kigali, or Bujumbura.

With the time and resources college provided, Hughbert took his coding game even further. He founded TimeTrax, a business which specialized in the web development skills that made him money with the 106 and Park site. This time around, Hughbert was helping businesses market themselves better. On top of the coding, Hughbert was a successful small-scale stock trader, making a ten percent margin on nearly everything in his portfolio.

I was blown away by what he showed me every time I visited his basement dwelling². Three screens full of coding projects, tutorials, and online magic tricks that Hughbert had a way of making simple. Depending on the day, I'd learn something that unlocked like fifteen new ideas. It was liberating to find out most custom website layouts come in pre-coded packages that sold for under $50. I learned of sites that sold you ad space on related websites for under $100. Adding functions like fading images and cool sidebar effects was as simple as downloading what are called plugins and uploading them to your site. Things that were simple to him but life-changing in the right hands. If you were curious enough to get Hughbert talking about tech innovation for five minutes, you'd eventually hear something that made you feel like you could hang with Mark Zuckerberg.

The optimism that international students, especially my Ugandan friends, brought to their college experience was refreshing. These people came thousands of miles from their homes to get an educational, social, and cultural experience that billions around the world coveted. An experience that many immigrants—my parents—risked arrest and death for. Simply looking around at one another reminded them of that fact. Coming to the United States as an international student wasn't as dangerous, but everyone at the African Apartments understood the value of being on American soil.

Being around Hughbert and all of his peers gave me alternate pairs of eyes to see the world through. It was so much more beautiful. Their gratitude wasn't excessive—homework, exams, and professors pissed them off like any student—but it was always present. The default attitude many American students had toward college life was "could be better." But a drink in hand and some Pallaso or Wizkid playing on a Friday night, and your stress suddenly seemed out of place.

I continued to roll through Gauthier's place on various weekends, going out and meeting other guys in and around the apartments. We'd go to house parties or to Brit's Pub and watch soccer. I continued to hang out at Hughbert's apartment, a symbiotic relationship where knowledge and skills flowed back and forth in equilibrium. If my social life at St. Thomas was Google Maps, the African Apartments was a saved destination. By the time Gauthier and Marshall both moved out after finishing their Master's programs, I was already an established community member.

I could stroll by at any odd hour and get a warm greeting from Roger or Wassua. I could knock on Hughbert's ground level window and wake him up from an afternoon nap. It was a neighborhood within the neighborhood. It was an insulated world that kept parts of my identity healthy and growing while I moved through the heavy atmosphere of the greater world of St. Thomas.

9

Tweak

...

"People indulge in drug culture when their reality is trash."

Briana's stark observation continues to resonate with me. Drugs can be the air under your wings during an emotional high. Drugs can also be the ball and chain clamped to your leg as you drown in the murky, suffocating depth of your subconscious. Swimming in those dark waters are fears and anxieties. In the mind of a college student, those concerns might be the transition into adulthood, or newfound vulnerability in a poorly-defined intimate relationship. Along with those common growing pains, bigger questions like, "Who am I in this place?" and, "How do I exist here?" could be found ominously cruising through the minds of some Black students at St. Thomas.

College is a place for people to figure out how they'll fit in the world. But I, and countless other black and brown St. Thomas students before me, had to figure out how to fit into college first. If you weren't involved on campus at St. Thomas, you were invisible. If you were involved, you had to fight to understand White students more than they struggled to understand you. A classmate might say racialized police brutality is overblown, and no one would challenge it. A "friend" might be surprised you aren't a scholarship athlete. People anonymously posted things like, "Wow, so many Black people on campus. Don't like it," on the social media platform YikYak[1] (back when it was relevant), and you'd be left wondering how many of your fellow students agreed.

Individually, these were instances you could move past. Over time though, they drained you. My friends and I smoked weed as an escape from the bullshit. But as quickly as it made me fly, weed was just as liable to drown me if I wasn't paying attention.

I've never hit rock bottom due to drugs, nor have I seen anyone I know hit such a low. But I've seen the descent, the wrong turn taken. An uncomfortable four-minute laugh attack off a strong bong hit[2] becoming lethargy the next day, and academic probation a couple of months after. Boredom turned into casual Xannie use, leaving the user with short-term memory loss and a constant out-of-it look. Depression turned into a bad acid trip, which prompted leaving the state of Minnesota altogether. I myself have been taken down the wrong path by a substance. I've tweaked before.

The release I experienced that summer night smoking weed with Philipo wasn't a good release. That's what tweaking is, the mind unleashed for the worse. Sometimes the pack had me feeling like Black Jimmy Neutron, epiphanies and ideas hitting me like a classic "Brain blast!" during my high. But this time, thoughts unraveled in my mind's eye like an animation of DNA being unzipped. My mind left me, and I left my body.

Dull streetlights and gentle warmth bathed the night. As Philipo and I chatted over a blunt, my mind grappled with concepts of racial identity and manhood. They eluded me, melting from solid truths into fluid concepts. Sometimes they evaporated into airy thoughts I couldn't hold onto depending on what I was thinking about. I thought about my parents being Ethiopian and how that meant two different things for them and me. My disconnect from parts of their culture made me feel like I could never be whole. Like my outer self didn't really present my inner self, like an egg that has peanut butter inside instead of yolk.

Weed was a hyperactive enzyme in my head. It was at its worst that night, breaking down my identity into fragments, obsessively rearranging the pieces in search of the perfect whole. Perfection never came, so it kept at it, getting faster as it went. Thoughts started flying like debris in my mental tornado, my self-perception ripped to shreds swirling around itself. Sharp images quickly flashed in the chaos, including one where my Blackness was a mask that eight-year-old Zander had to wear once he moved from snow-white Sioux Falls to St. Paul. The mask was one with my skin at some parts, stapled on at others, and disconnected from the remaining spaces of my face. I couldn't tell if it was meant to be a part of me or not. It freaked me the fuck out.

While my quarter-life identity crisis attacked, Philipo went on about the majesty of planet Earth's lifeforms. I tried to get a grip on creation, destruction, rebirth and the scope of time Earth operates on and how-infinitesimally-small-our-scope-of-time-is-relative-to-that-and-why-our-lives-still-mattered-in-the-universal-chain-of-events-no-matter-how-quickly-we-come-and-go-I-wanted-to-do-something-but-I-couldn't-figure-it-out-because-my-face-was-crack-ing-and-falling-apart-and-my-soul-was-looking-for-a-new-body-I-think-I-see-infinity-it-feels-like-I-been-there-but-gotta-go-through-somethin-to-get-back-there-that-Theo-lecture-on-Hinduism-may-be-right-this-could-be-karmic-responsibility-I-could-be-aaaaaaaa....

THUMP

I'M GOOD, I'm good. I'm back...whoa.

The back of my head was warm with numbed pain. I had passed out and fell backwards onto the cement in the alley outside of Philipo's apartment building. I faced the blunt too quickly, over-charging my thoughts in the process. My attempt at keeping up with the whirlwind left me ungrounded. I forgot how to balance. I felt trapped in a slow motion reality on the way down, too gone to do anything about my temporarily limp body. The thud of my land-ing jolted me back into myself.

The street lights hovering above us gently welcomed me back to the quiet evening. Philipo was crouched over me, baffled as to what went wrong. He helped me up from the ground and back toward the apartment. Rattled, I tried to explain the incident to Philipo as we walked down some stairs into the courtyard. Dis-tracted by my own blathering, I landed awkwardly on a step and sprained my ankle. I assured him I was good. I wasn't.

I was nearly brought to tears later that night reflecting on the experience. How lost do you have to be to let go of your mind? Weed was great when it wasn't steering your thoughts into the depths of your anxieties at rocket speed in search of answers, but it was persistent when it did. Too persistent. Without control, your stream of consciousness powered by weed tries to find the ultimate conclusion to anything and everything. Some people fall off the ride along the way and chill, a phenomenon called being "stuck," just watching thoughts go by. But for someone like me, someone who lived in his head, I felt obligated to follow.

Weed, and drugs in general, aren't like that for everyone. They do different things to different people, and different things to the same person in different times of their life. In my experience, mental and emotional health largely determines where a buzz or a trip takes you. The slow but steady drag of St. Thomas' campus climate put my mental health in a surprisingly shaky state the night of my only tweak moment.

Black and African folks, especially men, tend to glance over mental health symptoms. I was no different, writing off my obsessive worries as "deep thinking" for months. Since I was highly functional, active, and happy around my friends, it took a while to admit I was struggling with how I felt about myself. But relative to a couple of other Black male peers, I had it under control. Most memorable was the suffering of Darrell, the nerdy, snowbunny-loving philosopher from inner-city Omaha.

Darrell and I shared a class together the semester before he transferred out of St. Thomas. It was "Race and Ethnicity" with none other than Buffy Smith. Given the relatable professor, and course content right up his alley, it was hard to understand why Darrell rarely did his homework or participated in class. Smoking sessions with him and Philipo revealed a deeper disengagement, a failure to connect with anyone at St. Thomas outside of his daily smoking partners.

Around Philipo and I, Darrell was a source of unbridled energy. His wild stream of consciousness ramblings turned any ordinary topic—lunch, the weather, a new haircut, anything—into huge conversations about the progress of humanity. You could show him a new 2 Chainz song, and soon you'd be talking about the historical significance of percussion in Black music. He'd be liable to turn that into a comparison between music and math, and get irritated that more Black people aren't comfortable with math. Meanwhile, the only thing you remembered asking Darrell is, "Yo, you heard 2 Chainz's new shit?"

But around acquaintances and other students, Darrell often seemed turned off, sullen even. Passionate run-on sentences were swapped for terse replies and forgettable conversations. Johnny, Philipo and several other friends also noticed these changes in Darrell's demeanor. Whatever issues I had fitting in and staying sane at St. Thomas were affecting Darrell doubly hard. I could only imagine what it was like for him on his acid trip.

Darrell, Philipo, and a friend of ours named Devin were set on tripping one day. Fall semester was nearing its end, it was snowy and cold, and there wasn't much to be responsible for. For Philipo and Devin, this was the perfect time to try a psychedelic. For Darrell, who had tripped on acid once before, it was the perfect time to lose himself.

Devin was an energetic dude two years our junior who went to Century College. Knowing his goofy ass was going to be there along with Philipo's optimistic and adventurous persona balanced my anxiety over Darrell's hyper-abstract and neurotic thinking patterns. Devin brought the 25i, an acid alternative, in the form of small, translucent slips of soaked paper called tabs. Before placing the tabs on their tongues and beginning their trips, Devin, Philipo, and Darrell wanted me to supervise them at Philipo's place.

An hour into their trips, Philipo and Devin were peaceful as could be. Philipo just sat on his black wooden coffee table, chuckled every so often, and walked around a bit. Devin lay face down on the floor with a couch pillow, almost asleep. Darrell though...

While Philipo and Devin chilled, Darrell stared at the ceiling as he sank into the couch, vocalizing his thoughts in a stream of consciousness fashion. It sounded robotic though, not the eager monologues we were used to hearing from him. Darrell periodically went quiet, seemingly trying to keep up with himself. Then he started getting wide-eyed. He'd flail his limbs every so often and emit some sharp, high-pitched "AAH"s that Philipo was not enjoying at all. Two hours in, Darrell started walking around trying to ask for things but stopping halfway through. He was also trying to explain his experience but couldn't finish his sentences. His mind was moving too fast.

Darrell wanted some air. He stumbled past me to the apartment door and started spinning himself along the wall with his arms fully extended. His gaze was well beyond where I was. He was completely gone. It was like communicating with a zombie who had moments of genius. I grabbed his shoulder and suggested we go back inside. He silently agreed and turned back with me.

During the latter half of the trip, Darrell and Philipo wanted me to play some music. We couldn't get through thirty seconds of a song without Darrell or Philipo making fast circular gestures with their index fingers and snapping, "Change it!" at me. Their requests had an alarming urgency to them, as if they were on the verge of a breakdown. This part was funny. It seemed like they got trapped in the rhythm or loop of a track way quicker than they should have. They calmed down after some minutes of this and began the process of coming down.

Once Darrell could say more than, "AAH," and, "Change it!" he started explaining his experience to me. He said his thoughts had no context, that they were stripped of common terms and definitions used to label our thoughts and feelings. Darrell's greatest example was his time spent in front of Philipo's bathroom mirror. He was so detached from his senses that his own reflection caused him confusion. Anxiety, even. His mind was tied down to nothing, not even a sense of self-recognition. It was a mental departure far more serious than the one I experienced with Philipo. The fact that neither Philipo nor Devin experienced as much of an escape during their acid trips that day was a testament to how far gone Darrell already was prior to his trip.

These experiences weren't life or death. And in the grand scheme of things, substances weren't a defining part of my college journey. But they shined a bright light on the personal struggles that did define it. People don't go out of their way to help someone who seems a bit lost, especially if you're broke and not White. The lack of formal guidance at St. Thomas left us responsible for our own coping mechanisms and creating our own space to process. It's why Darrell and I had our tweak moments[3] in and around Philipo's crib, a safe place for our minds to wade into the deep end.

Our episodes brought both Darrell and I to hard realizations about our self-perception. I found it okay to admit that being Black in a space like St. Thomas was stressful. During our chat years later, Darrell told me the trip was a turning point for him. He realized he wasn't ready to embrace the social challenges St. Thomas presented.

Sadly, even the pull of uplifting spirits like Buffy and Miss Vivian weren't enough in cases like Darrell's. He moved back to Omaha to finish his undergraduate degree shortly after, regaining the confidence and optimism he had before coming to St. Thomas. Given time, St. Thomas inevitably defeated a number of promising brown-skinned men such as the former Chief Diversity Officer, Darrell, the guy that couldn't stop laughing after a bong hit, and several others that I knew. Drugs didn't start it, and they weren't a major reason for their failure to adapt. But they gave us a peek into what was really troubling us, and that view was often painful.

10

Nigga

● ● ●

What is this chapter gonna be about? Nigga, I'ont know. But imagine two young niggas who just got to college flirting with this White girl, right? They're friends so they're talkin' shit doin' what young niggas do when out of nowhere...*leans in, whispers* ...one of them says the n-word.

"Tsk, niggas."

"I'm sayin' tho."

Then the White girl goes, "Could you please not use that word? I get offended when I hear it."

Girl, *whet?*

"Wait...how are *you* offended by *us* saying the n-word among ourselves?" Matt asked, appropriately.

"It's not that, I just think that the word in general is really negative and I just don't like hearing it used by anyone."

So there we were, Matt and I, offended that this White woman was offended by *us* saying 'nigga' thinking she was doing us a favor by taking offense to it. This scene is only the tip of the iceberg. Sadly, young Black Minnesotans know a thing or two about White people's nauseating obsession with the politics of 'nigga'.

Discussing 'nigga' with White people is rarely productive. Like the White student in the scene above, some have a gag reflex to anything that has to do with the word. *Bad word! Stay away! I'm not racist!* It's like discussing sex with a teen from a highly conservative religious background whose sex education consists of, "No."

To the overzealous (typically White) person, 'nigga' seems like a powerful toy. Like a cool outdated weapon that just *needs* to be played with. The thing about outdated weapons, however, is that they're still weapons. The defiance and self-determined cool that young Black folk packed into those five letters does not wash away the centuries of vitriolic oppression inherited from its –er ending parent word. Mishandling 'nigga' is playing with an old grenade: it seems safe to toss around now, but it's actually *way* more unpredictable. With Tom Hanks' son and Bill Maher as the best recent examples, White people tend not to know what they're playing with when using 'nigga'.

'Nigga' embodies a 400-year-old power struggle, the Black-White race and class dynamic the United States is founded upon. Claiming your share of 'nigga' is American tradition, right up there with fireworks on the 4th of July and buying into the American Dream. Much like the American Dream, everyone wants to view themselves as both one with the oppressed and as one with the powerful. You want to have enough clout to say 'nigga', but also appear to be someone who understands what it feels like to be called a nigger. You know, Jim Crow edition, maybe even *Adventures of Huckleberry Finn* flavored. The type of 'nigger' chanted at someone's great-grandfather before the noose got tight. *Nigger.*

Did you feel the difference between how I spoke of 'nigga' versus how I spoke of 'nigger'? Those who play the all-American game of power don't associate the meaning of the latter with the former. But those who see 'nigga' as 'nigger' with a face lift associate the same hateful degradation with both terms. Even within racial groups, there are too many different beliefs about the terms to come to any reasonable consensus on it.

More Americans want a piece of 'nigga' than they do of any other word. And no one likes admitting that people, not dictionaries, decide the meanings of words. People have to create and normalize words before they are given an official place in our language. It's why 'binge-watch' and 'tech-savvy', for example, are now in the Oxford English Dictionary. No one wants to contest the meaning and usage of 'nigger' since White supremacists have it on lock. But there are a number of different people that consider themselves worthy shareholders of 'nigga'.

Latino-Americans and Asian-Americans who think they identify with the racial and class struggles of Black Americans claim the word. Black teens and young adults struggling to grasp their Blackness within White peer groups use the word to gain control of their racial identities. Black elders who have achieved middle-middle class status or above try to shake off a painful past by placing stigma on the word. White fans of hip-hop, no matter how casual, claim the word in an attempt to feel like a truer member of the culture. Lower class White people trying to survive within Black peer groups also claim the word.

In many ways, oppression is viewed as a source of authority. Aligning with the Black American struggle is a popular way of tapping into that source, and 'nigga' is the simplest tool to do it with. But with so many people making claims to 'nigga', no one can truly regulate it. So here we are today, where every event, hood, hangout, comment section, and person is a potential landmine that triggers at the sound of 'nigga'. If we're being honest about this country's social context, no one has the ability to give a simple 'yes' or 'no' to the question of, "Are (insert group of people) allowed to say the word?" All we can really say is tread lightly, and be aware of the minefield that you walk on daily.

The pressure points of this minefield are identifiable. Some can be sneaky though, like that White girl Matt and I were talking to. As a Black person, you also have to know your own pressure points. Sometimes, you have to be the mine. Ecuadorian homie says 'nigga'? Let it slide. Arab dude hanging with the Somali guys says 'nigga'? Detonate. Ridicule him to make sure he stays in check, but don't blow him all the way up. Being mindful of when, where, why, and how you say or discuss 'nigga' applies to everyone, but mostly to White people. Especially to this one White girl at this one event I was at this one time. She didn't even *actually* say the word and shit still went down.

Troubling Waters was a series ran by the American Culture and Difference department meant for the school's cultural enrichment. The namesake was a biblical reference to John 5:4 made by former St. Thomas professor Bill Banfield:

For an angel went down at a certain season into the pool, and troubled the water: whosoever then first after the troubling of the water stepped in was made whole of whatsoever disease he had.

By stirring the pot and discussing controversial topics, faculty and students hoped to make whole those who stepped into the troubled water. Typically, there were a couple of presenters, one faculty, and one or two students. Today, however, Dr. David Todd Lawrence of the English department was our angel diving into the proverbial water. The discussion was about the word 'nigga'.

Dr. Lawrence went by Todd and was on first-name basis with anyone on campus he ever had a conversation with. He was a bit taller than me, sturdily built with these can't-miss freeform dreadlocks that looked like a Basquiat painting on colonialism. They contained the struggle, the resistance, the oppression, *and* the freedom. Those locks were tough, I'm telling you. Like peaceful yet powerful branches on a Black Power tree.

A humble, well-read man, Todd was known to have calm, considerate insight on even the most polarizing issues. His stance on 'nigga' was no different. "No one can just ban the word. White people can use it if they want," he said to the ire of some 'nigga' purists. "But they have to accept all potential consequences depending on who they're using the word around." This thoughtful tree-like being of a man tried to lead the bumbling group of 70ish undergrad students toward progressive race relations that day. It didn't work.

The lecture got under way, and it wasn't long before a brave White girl asked the burning question dozens of her counterparts were probably too scared to ask themselves.

"I get that the word is a term of endearment when Black people use it with each other. So what's wrong with White people saying it? Is it okay if we use it?"

"IS IT OKAY THAT YOU'RE PEOPLE ENSLAVED MY PEOPLE 400 YEARS AGO?"

Enter Tobias, a light-skinned school football player who felt empowered off the strength of a White privilege discussion the day before. Landmine.

Tobias was heated. He stood and turned around to stare down what he imagined was the White Devil in that auditorium. Brave White girl instantly got defensive, then Tobias passionately claimed ownership of the word 'nigga' and referred to, "my boy Tavion" (Tavier, it was Tavier, and we wanted to laugh but it was too tense) as an example of someone he'd use the word with. The nine other Black people present raised their hands, trying to side with Tobias without sounding like Malcolm X on a bad day. Soon, Brave White girl started crying because for all we know, she could have just wanted permission to sing along to Kanye's "New Slaves" without censoring herself.

It was awful. Myself and a couple other friends got the discussion onto some kind of productive course, making the issue about individual social realities and how Black people have different views on the word depending on their age, location, and social experiences. After the partially salvaged discussion ended, Todd went to console Brave White girl and get her and Tobias to make up with each other.

As we reflected on the incident two years later, Tobias told me he regretted how he behaved. But not because of what he said, but for his approach. He described himself as moving back and forth between the extremes of Black people who didn't give a fuck about race, and the Black people that couldn't talk about anything else. "Reputation matters, and I don't want mine to be a negative one," Tobias said admittedly.

I remember Tobias telling me and several other Black students about his view on racial justice. He explained his willingness to play the token Black guy amongst his popular White friends as a quest to "beat them at their own game." Getting high-profile finance internships despite finance not being his passion. Earning student leadership positions for the sake of clout. To Tobias, success in the system was a valid way of beating it.

Tobias hated that his White peers didn't understand the outcry over racialized police brutality. He hated that some of his White peers were comfortable saying 'nigga' to him and around him. But for the most part, he refrained from going off on people to preserve his status. At what cost? I'm not sure. But in talking to him, I knew his situation was more complex than a Black guy looking for his Black card. Tobias' explosion at Troubling Waters was brash and ill-timed, but it was genuinely him.

Tobias told me his godfather called him out about his approach once. His godfather was concerned Tobias was shunning his true self to prove himself to those that didn't respect him. That conversation helped Tobias admit how unhealthy it was to play the game he was playing. Suppressing how he felt about casually racist White friends polarized his view of racial justice activism, and sometimes made him highly sensitive to conversations about race like at Troubling Waters.

Tobias told me as he continues his journey into adulthood, he's still learning how to approach issues of race in more constructive ways. "Whatever my input is, I want someone to feel like they can have an honest input rather than people getting defensive and backtracking." Troubling Waters was an awkward moment, but it seems like it helped him learn some things about himself.

The development of racial identity can be a bitch when someone's social surroundings change. A Black American living in New Zealand would have an altered view of what their Blackness means there versus what it means in the United States. On a domestic scale, a Black girl from a Black neighborhood entering a mostly White four-year college will likely feel isolated due to her race for the first time in her life. But then there are Black people going from White to Black social environments rather than the other way around. They go through some weird shit.

Black Americans living abroad, as well as Black youth from neighborhoods of color going to college, learn different things about how Blackness is perceived. But many Black people coming from White worlds are *just* beginning to realize they are seen as Black by the outside world when they encounter more Black people. This tends to scare them away from digging further into racial identity, or radicalizes their view of race relations from Kumbaya to "Fuck White people." In my experience, this can apply to anyone considered a person of color in the United States who did not confront the fact that they're seen as such until their environment changed.

Though Tobias has racial awareness, I feel like he didn't really deal with his own place in a racialized world until college. What I witnessed was simply the beginning of that tricky process.

The debate around the word 'nigga' embodies a lot of our current issues discussing racial equity. It's hypersensitive, White people are clueless, Black people are the default authorities, and other people of color try to claim some of the authority without offending their Black counterparts. The debate is about language, about what a word means to different people. The subjectivity of the debate exposes how diverse opinions and beliefs within racial groups can be.

You can be Tobias and firmly believe in banning White people from using the word. You can be the White girl that Matt and I debated and believe no one should use the word. You can be like me and think it's all up to an individual's social reality, and in rare cases, a White person might actually own the word more genuinely than a Black person. You ever see the video of the White boy yelling, "Today I got time cuz!" in anticipation of a fight[1]? Yeah, he says 'nigga' more convincingly than a lot of Black suburbanites I know. I was shook.

It takes patience to sort out a mess like this. If race relations are a puzzle, we can't throw pieces out just because they look weird. Some opinions on 'nigga' confuse the hell out of me, but there's something valuable in every perspective that helps us see the issue more clearly. And please, White readers, don't make this chapter an invitation to troll me on Twitter or during a Q&A session.

11

Public Safety

• • •

One advantage of a small private school's campus climate is its safety. Unlike the sprawling campuses of state schools that blend into the commotion of a city, St. Thomas was insulated by trees, signs, and security technology. There was a stark difference in atmosphere between the edge of campus and its immediate surroundings. In a three-minute walk away from campus, the emergency lights, cameras, and assumed presence of school safety officials disappeared. Exposure and unpredictability set in. Opportunistic broke boys became muggers and robbers at three in the morning. Women, even in broad daylight, became bigger targets of sexual harassment and assault off campus than they already were on campus.

In many ways, the on-campus college lifestyle at four-year schools exists in a bubble. Children who are considered legal adults get to feel like responsible, independent people and still depend on their institution (and oftentimes their parents) for everything. I'm not making the all-millennials-are-babies argument, I know many college students to be resourceful and successfully independent. I mean, look at me. What I'm saying is there isn't much from the outside world that can affect your quality of life when a college campus is your home.

St. Thomas was a planet, and its atmosphere was made up of three elements: residence life, the student center, and Public Safety. Core human life necessities including food, shelter, hygiene, and social activity were taken care of by the first two elements. Public safety acted as the outermost layer under which everything else existed in peace. News of late night crimes and inner-city struggles burned up in the atmosphere like meteors entering Earth. By the time they landed, most threats were insignificant.

Students in the bubble were left with no good reason to care about what went on beyond it. But the meteors of unpleasant worldly events did real damage to nearby planets. The Midway neighborhood. East Side Saint Paul. North Minneapolis. Latino families in South Minneapolis trying to get DREAMers into college. These planets got rocked often. Life still goes on in these resilient worlds, but it was always disappointing to me that such a protected, well-off community like St. Thomas didn't take the time to acknowledge its neighbors.

Now that you understand how stable and removed St. Thomas' campus environment is, you'll understand what makes Public Safety such a strange entity. One requirement for a college or university's campus safety department is effective communication. At St. Thomas, Public Safety sent alerts straight to people's emails once an incident was reported, or straight to the phone via text if it was urgent. This was helpful in keeping the community aware of neighborhood crimes and repeat offenders of those crimes. It also helped the St. Paul and Minneapolis police departments do their jobs when they came around to investigate.

The community benefitted from Public Safety alerts, but they were frustrating to read if you were a Black male. For one, Black guys on campus were scarce, and suspects were often, unfortunately, Black guys. Even a mild correlation to a recent suspect description could implicate you enough to catch a probing glare or two. Secondly, the types of offenses these Black men committed were fucking ridiculous. They were crimes, yes, but strange in a way that made you ask, "Why, just why?"

At least several times a semester, Abeye and I would see messages from Public Safety at the top of our inboxes while chilling in the student center. We would shake our heads and chuckle in anticipation, *praying* some goofy-ass nigga who vaguely resembled either of us or our friends didn't do something stupid. This is what we read once:

"Public Safety would like to inform the University of St. Thomas community of several groping/attempted groping incidents near campus."

How are you caught just *attempting* to—never mind. What happened?

On 02/08/2016 at approximately 1:00 PM, a UST student reported she was walking back to campus along Cleveland Avenue. A male suspect approached the student and began making unwanted advances towards her. As the student approached the Signal Care Auto Garage, the suspect stated he was going to grab the stu-

dent's buttocks. The student then got the attention of an employee at Signal Care, went inside, and called the St. Paul Police Department. The suspect continued north along Cleveland Avenue, but then turned and fled southbound on foot."

...The fuck?! Did that play out in your head like it did in mine? In public, at one o'clock in the afternoon?

The suspect has been described as a Black male approximately 6'0" - 6'4" with a thin build, wearing glasses, with dreadlocks pulled into a ponytail.

Weeell damn. Abeye and I had a friend named Herbert with long dreads. Abeye himself had dreads, as well as glasses. Another friend of ours named Hamza had dreads too, plus he pushed six feet. While our would-be buttocks groper sprinted down the block in failure, he earned some dirty looks for Hamza and Herbert from several White female students later that day.

It wasn't simply the suspect being identified as Black that upset me. If it was true, it was true. But if my friends were invisible when greeting a White girl passing by on an average day, they could *not* be missed if she was on the lookout for a Black guy striving to grab some ass in public. Ridiculous, but as far as some White girls are concerned, that may as well be one of the God-given purposes of Black men. Eternally asking how she got all of that in them jeans. Going dumb for the bum. Booty predators, or something like that, right Mrs. Clinton? Even if these thoughts were not front and center in a prejudiced White mind, they had to be the subconscious base of any belief about Black men being hypersexual.

Though it seemed like the only accomplishment of that report was the further vilification of Black men, I can't undermine the value of such reports for women in the community. Reports of groping and other forms of sexual misconduct came often. Black female friends of mine that talked about these alerts with me confirmed the frequency with which public sexual harassment happened. They also understood it didn't take much for the unsavory narrative of one random yet nearby Black man to be applied to other Black men within a closed off, cotton-white community like St. Thomas. Our dreadheaded groper peer was probably the most prominent story about a Black person many White students at St. Thomas read that week.

Public Safety did a good job of providing descriptors outside of the basic physical characteristics, but it wasn't always enough to keep people from being racially profiled. You thought Hamza receiving bothered stares was bad. Consider how offensive it would be to someone like my man Todd—a tenured professor in his thirteenth year there at the time—to be questioned by a Public Safety officer about his involvement in a crime reported earlier in the day. Someone had tipped them off about a dreadheaded fellow walking around campus…oops?

The trend of unusual Public Safety reports involving Black male suspects didn't stop after I graduated. I went to an on-campus event almost a year after graduating, and a friend of mine was catching me up on last semester's highlights. He then checked his email on his phone. A Public Safety alert was one of the unread messages:

On 02/01/2017 at approximately 02:40 PM, a St. Thomas student reported that an unidentified male had entered her room. The student confronted the male who was rummaging through her drawers. The male claimed to be a University of St. Thomas student. The suspect returned a charger he had taken out of the student's drawer and left the room.

The suspect was a Black male approximately 5' to 6', approximately 180 pounds, 25 to 35 years of age, shaved head, thin framed glasses, thin black mustache, wearing a black jacket, black stocking cap, black pants, black belt, cellphone case on hip, black boots, and carrying a black duffle bag with white Air Jordan logo on it. The suspect smelled of heavy smoke.

Experiencing the monthly comedy of St. Thomas Public Safety reports as a student convinced me these messed-up descriptions of Black suspects really *did* happen often. It still didn't prepare me for how crazy this one was. Five feet to…six feet? But the same weight either way? So a short guy built like a bowling ball? Or someone tall and well built? Also, considering how vague the actual shape and size of said person is, where did the rest of these acute descriptors come from? If camera footage was used to get those finer details, how the hell do you end up with such a useless height and weight description?

There's no way the description of this man's stature was done with accuracy in mind. Even if we relied on the accessories, it wasn't uncommon to see a brown-skinned person on campus wearing most of those things to and from the gym. Not casting the net wide at all, are we?

The suspect description wasn't the only bewildering thing in the report. The awkward description of the incident made me admit to myself that men, including Black men, did a lot of stupid shit at the expense of women. My initial reaction was to burst into laughter at the thought of a grown ass Black man panicking at the site of a shocked, most likely White, female St. Thomas student. The exchange must have been the strangest conversation either of them had all week. And of all the things to be caught red-handed stealing, a phone charger? Really? That's what you wandered onto a campus and broke into a dorm room for?

I finally concluded the people who get into these situations were the most peculiar characters I've ever read about—aside from stories with "Florida Man" headlines. Why, just why is this guy dressed black-on-black-on-black-on-black down to the goddamn cellphone case? And who uses *those* anymore?! This man woke up and decided the look of the day was "shady." He was basically begging to be profiled. On top of that, it didn't even serve the purpose of making him stealthier. Much like Failed Dreadhead Groper guy, this nigga was walking around campus bold as hell in the middle of the afternoon trying to commit crime in a street ninja winter outfit.

I was conflicted. I didn't know whether to direct the bulk of my frustration at Public Safety, sheltered White people (which typically included Public Safety), or a few wayward Black men. As much as I want people to see the five-to-six-foot failed burglar as comical, it must be frightening as a woman to encounter a random man in your room. But given the overwhelmingly negative portrayals of Black men in American media, seeing such a careless description about the suspect's stature was bound to trigger me. Even if the only source of info was a girl in a state of fear, you'd think she could do better than a twelve-inch height range and the entire spectrum of body types.

Reading about the all-black-everything struggle burglar made me reminisce on all of the equally confusing Public Safety reports I saw while in college. One alert was of a Black man who walked up to a St. Thomas employee in the Minneapolis skyway, punched him in the face, and fled[1]. There were no details about what could have triggered this *Grand Theft Auto* version of assault. There were also a couple of indecent exposure reports where two different White men in the same week drove up to female St. Thomas students, flashed their dicks out the window, and drove off. I was disgusted, amused by the pointlessness, and thankful they weren't Black. The gratefulness was short-lived since reports of "normal" crimes like muggings and armed robberies came in semi-frequently. *Those* suspects were Black.

Looking back, each memorable incident report deserved to be taken seriously by the St. Thomas community. They also helped me see how clueless I was about the level of danger faced by women daily. But while Public Safety was keeping the bubble world of St. Thomas safe, any brown-skinned man within it could be considered a threat in a moment's notice. So when stories of the unpredictable world beyond the bubble constantly implicated Black men, it was hard for me to not treat those stories with defensive humor. It's how I coped with knowing that a Ph.D. and a great track record didn't exempt Dr. Lawrence from being a no-name suspect at his place of employment. It's how I brushed off the time James Thomas and I were locked out of a media lab on campus, and the Public Safety officer I called over questioned James' status as a student.

During my time as a St. Thomas student, Public Safety kept me safe. It also didn't. The department gave me a couple of rides home, retrieved a lost item for me, and cast suspicion on people I cared about. Sometimes we're so caught up in having an either/or conclusion, we're unable to accept when a situation is and/also. Like many other parts of my St. Thomas experience, Public Safety both harmed and helped me.

12

10 Deep

•••

Once I had friends who understood the constant drag of racial tension at St. Thomas, I warmed up to the idea of going to St. Thomas parties. At this point, we understood the issue with St. Thomas' social scene wasn't simply White people: it was a high concentration of upper class and rural White people from the Midwest that hadn't experienced anything outside of their bubbles. The only things challenging them to see the world differently at St. Thomas were ten young niggas walking up to a house party with a redheaded Australian kid from Boston.

Like any good group of college partygoers, we pregamed before making the brave trips that became a weekly routine. Even in the oversized pack that was our friend group at the time, you didn't walk into a house full of non-city Minnesotans without having alcohol in you. It wasn't a requirement unless you *actually* want to enjoy yourself in that environment.

For one, the drinking starts earlier in Minnesota than most places. Not only do parties end at disappointing hours, there's usually not shit else to do when it gets dark at 5:00 p.m. for half the school year. Ice, snow, and biting windchill were always ready to beat your ass outside, so the false warmth alcohol provided gave us the courage to move to and from these parties. Wow, what a depressing picture of a social life I just painted.

Attending a house party at St. Thomas meant walking into a house full of people who were: (i) trapped indoors with a bunch of alcohol (ii) socially inhibited Monday through Friday 9-5, and (iii) only knew how to be outgoing and honest—especially around people of color—when they drink. Between the fake-deep heart-to-heart conversations, bad dancing, or lack of dancing, haphazard playlists with a surprising amount of hip-hop, and the occasional dubstep-hip-hop remix to spice things the fuck up, trust me, you wanted to be *at least* strongly buzzed.

Parties at St. Thomas had my friends and I out of our element, but we had to make the best of it. Despite the occasionally foolish attempts at wooing White women, James Thomas' approach to social life at St. Thomas was admirable. Much like Muhdi before us, James saw racial lines, but he also looked above them. The optimism and the determination of James made me realize the twofold nature of acknowledging racial differences. On one hand, you'd be a fool not to adjust to the subtle but clear distinction in how you're perceived as a Black person in a White space. No, don't say 'nigga' casually to your White acquaintances. Yes, the hair you spend hours on maintaining might get called "unprofessional" or, for better or (probably) worse, stir up a frenzy of onlookers begging to pet you.

On the other hand, to use racial and cultural differences as the reason for your unhappiness in a White space is self-limiting. It was a good excuse back when your very presence as a Black person evoked death threats, and life certainly isn't *easier* when Black in America. But the difference between my peers who constantly noted that and those who didn't was marked. Those who were more selective about the racial issues they dove into seemed happier. Interactions with them were less draining. More mental energy was spent on improving personal well-being than explaining why doing so as a person of color was a difficult task.

Often, those of my friends who picked and chose their racial battles actively fought against racial inequities by being their best selves. They became resident advisors and orientation leaders to add racial diversity to student leadership. They worked to fix the racial achievement gap by becoming Dean's List students and getting into graduate schools. These students embodied the change they wanted to see at St. Thomas. And it's not like they frowned upon conventional activism, either. These students also kept up with popular racial justice readings and participated in racial justice protests on and off campus. Instead of striving to tell everyone how whack they thought St. Thomas was, they learned patience. They learned self-care. They elevated to a point where no one could simply dismiss them.

My friends and I got better at shrugging off race-based annoyances, but we still struggled in our early St. Thomas nightlife ventures. We were becoming more optimistic, but none of us really had the juice like that. We were still dismissible.

"We didn't have boats. We didn't have cabins. We didn't even have an off-campus place at the time." Talking to James Thomas years later made the truth of our ain't-shitness clear. Even when James and I eventually got places off campus, our friend group never had the status symbols our more popular White peers had.

We didn't know money. We didn't know expensive outdoor activities. In fact, a lot of us grew up ridiculing shit like skiing, boating, and cabin trips since we *knew* our parents would go broke trying to provide such experiences. So we just called it all "White people shit" and left it at that. Socializing at St. Thomas was a game that none of my Black peers were familiar with. Kinda like hockey, just out of our realm.

Since my friends and I couldn't compete with the preexisting advantages many St. Thomas students had, we had to become more involved on campus. Our early social struggles weren't just about us being Black. We were also...well, boring. Our days consisted of class, basketball, and video games. Hella fun, but we weren't really *doing* anything. We had to get jobs, join clubs, anything that got us off of our asses. We then had to befriend White folks who would then help us befriend other White folks. Simply put, we had to have more shit to talk about besides NBA 2K14 and racism. Evolving into unique, interesting people meant we had to stop scapegoating our skin color.

It didn't take long for the homies to get active. Johnny started running track, which came with all the social perks of being on a major school sports team. James started working at Student Diversity and Inclusion Services (SDIS), which set Abeye and I up for positions in the same office a year later. SDIS exposed us to students of color we didn't even know existed. The office also plastered our faces on the big digital ad screen in the ASC, which prompted random students to unexpectedly acknowledge us at times. Our group befriended Black women a class above us who ran the school dance club and knew their way around the party scene as well as anyone.

We were growing, meeting White people, and discovering small bands of other Black men and women like we were stumbling upon new civilizations. Simply getting out more resulted in more friends. Crazy, right? We went from gearing up to go to one house or one apartment to scrolling through our texts trying to decide in which order we wanted to attend the multitude of parties on any given Thursday, Friday, or Saturday.

Seeing the overwhelmed face of a party host when they laid eyes on the depth chart we called a friend group never really stopped. But between persistent partying and actually having lives on campus, it didn't take long for our faces to become recognizable. Soon we stopped creeping through rooms and standing at the fringes of beer pong games. We just stayed Black, mobbed, and talked to people. As parties go, that led us to more people. New acquaintances poured us up and smoked us up, so we returned the favor. We never openly acknowledged it, but wow. St. Thomas parties started to become fun for us.

As the parties got better, the stories in our post-game recaps did too. We still talked about pickup basketball games and complained about "White people shit," but it didn't consume us anymore. There were more stories of busted parties, embarrassing drunkenness, and the occasional "I can't believe this White girl actually twerked for me despite it being kinda weird" stories. A couple of times, the redheaded Bostonian Australian kid would bust out a bottle of liquor from his coat and be like, "Just snagged it from that one house," and we'd be like, "Bro, you stole an entire bottle and put it in your coat?" He baffled us[1], but we got laughs and free drinks out of it.

There were also more successes in our attempts to connect with girls. Naturally, there were also more failures, a good thing since it meant these interactions were coming more frequently. James Thomas and another friend dueled for the attention of a White girl they both met one night, ending with James dramatically yelling, "I LOVE YOU," on the walk back to campus as a last-ditch effort to beat out his competitor. It was *never* that serious for the rest of us, but it made for good drama.

Even if some of the stories weren't our proudest moments, we were having fun. We released the shackles of self-pity and started going in. Partying at St. Thomas forced us to put ourselves out there if we expected to get something good out of our time. Even if our initial attempts were clumsy, we eventually figured it out. We never quite stopped pulling up to parties deep as fuck, but we stopped caring about how it looked and started caring about talking to whoever. Drinking with whoever. Playing beer pong with whoever. We stuck out like a chocolate malt ball in vanilla ice cream, but we made it a strength rather than a liability. We embraced the curiosity instead of complaining about it. We learned how to make our own stories, and they were lit. Finally, we felt like St. Thomas students.

13

Reviving BESA

...

When the active Black community at your school—Black folks who hang with other Black folks and strongly identify with their Blackness—is like twenty people, graduating seniors can leave a sizeable dent. This is what happened when the Black Empowerment Student Alliance (BESA) reached the end of the academic season my first year at St. Thomas. The entire executive board (e-board) was a group of close classmates ready to bounce. BESA left with them, going defunct as soon as they graduated. Without the pulse of engaged students, BESA was pronounced dead. It seemed like no one at St. Thomas cared to bring it back to life until a group of four hesitant boys considered the possibility and said, "Aight, bet."

James Thomas was serious about creating a stronger Black presence on campus, one that would sustain itself after we graduated. One of the first things he did when he transferred to St. Thomas was ask Abeye about BESA, which led to some digging. With some help from SDIS, we learned Todd was the BESA faculty advisor, and that all it took was ten registered members to restart the club. Abeye, Johnny, James and I thought it was a worthwhile cause. Our decision to bring BESA back was the embodiment of a quote shown on a sign at the entrance of the ASC: *A society grows when people plant trees in whose shade they will never sit in.* Together, we actually cared enough to try leaving a mark at St. Thomas. It was quite the switch from the pessimism that defined my first year at the university.

"How many we get so far?"

"Six, including one Mexican girl."

"That's it? Where are all the Black people at?

"..."

The process was slow. My friends and I knew there was a large enough minority of frustrated students of color to create a BESA community. Getting them excited about it proved harder than it looked though. The same Black students that complained about the stifling racial ignorance on campus were too discouraged by their own experience to care about others. This is why many Black students moved around campus in small, isolated groups or by themselves. We all saw each other—we couldn't *not* see each other—but whether we crossed paths in the student center, or to and from class, no one tried to bridge the awkward gaps. We were too caught up in our own stories (hence this book, haha). It wasn't uncommon for me to meet a Black student for the first time despite knowing their name and seeing them on campus for months prior.

The Black student community at St. Thomas failed to meet my already lowered expectations. For one, a lot of Black students didn't even want a Black community. Many were school athletes and natives of Minnesota's more popular suburbs who identified too strongly with their White peers to join such a network. And among the Black students that did care to connect with racial peers, many felt content with keeping their heads down after making a few good friends.

Sure, a little squad might be all someone needed to get through college. But it wasn't solving the problem, just coping with it. Black students kept coming to St. Thomas, kept dealing with the same lack of support, and no one was doing shit about it. A unifying, student-led space like BESA was our best bet for a solution. Convincing all the fragmented cliques of this course of action took patience. But we persisted, and Abeye, James and I soon saw our black and brown peers drift to our table at the 2014 Activities Fair. Thirty registered members later, BESA was finally on the map at St. Thomas.

As BESA began its redefinition, so too did St. Thomas' administration. Jane Mulligan, the new president of the university, was entering her second year. Both a woman and unaffiliated with the Catholic Church—two firsts in the history of my highly progressive alma mater (lol)—President Mulligan was a symbol of progress the St. Thomas community found easy to attach to. Among her many vows to improve the university, she made it a point to connect with multicultural clubs continuing the fight for racial equity on campus. BESA was now included in that effort, and President Mulligan kept to her word. She was responsive to our emails, showed up to our events, and often stopped to chat with e-board members when she saw us on campus.

BESA hit the ground running that year. Our meetings, programs, and communications quickly developed a rhythm. Biweekly general meetings became highlights our members marked their calendars for. Social events like "BBQ and Bowling" drew dozens. Educational events like a workshop on racial identity development woke people up on campus and made Black students feel validated. Staff and faculty members like Miss Vivian and our advisor Todd relished the opportunities our events presented them to connect with a big group of young Black students.

Students of various Black backgrounds finally had a space where their opinions and experiences were the norm. The space we created for these Black students was a rare breath of fresh air in a suffocating atmosphere, away from the constant grating of campus-wide racial ignorance. Along with the emotional support we gave each other, we also learned from everyone's unique perspectives on Blackness. Hearing Somali folk, biracial Black people, Nigerian-Americans, Ethiopian-Americans, and recent arrivals from Kenya and Rwanda all speak on Black identity challenged everyone. It taught BESA members to accept different versions of the Black experience while fighting the same injustices together.

BESA's newfound popularity proved to us that St. Thomas, and college in general, certainly wasn't built with brown people in mind. Our programming was quality, but it wasn't the biggest reason for President Mulligan's piqued interest in us. The club's revival coincided with the national frenzy over racialized police brutality and Black Lives Matter. As universities heightened their sensitivity toward racial inequity, the organizing work of Black students warranted serious attention. Never before did students of color have such leverage within higher education. Now administrators *had* to care about what black and brown students did. When done right, a small group of young Black adults could submit a wealthy institution to national shame and jeopardize the jobs of negligent high-profile employees.

Our popularity was political, but it was a blessing. It meant the opportunities to make our presence felt on campus were enormous. BESA wanted Black students to be seen, heard, and supported in their pursuits by a university that continued to turn its back on them once they became students. The painful undercurrent of our message was the "trend" of dead young Black people highlighted by BLM. Our small effort made the pain seem less in vain.

We finally had the attention of the university. BESA was making waves, cutting through the flippant, cliquey feel of the general student club scene at St. Thomas. Our activity encouraged other multicultural student clubs to connect with us and each other. A typical walk from my dorm to the ASC pre-BESA used to consist of daydreaming and furtive glances at White students. Now? There was a familiar face at every turn. Not to mention the president of the whole goddamn place greeted me by my first name every time she saw me.

BESA's reintroduction was well received. My group of friends-turned-club-leaders finally started to make names for themselves amongst students, staff, and faculty. But we weren't really doing anything unique yet. We hadn't quite figured out how to leave our mark on campus, how to create a story that would make future Black students struggling at St. Thomas think, "Wow, they did that *here?*"

After the buzz of BESA's relaunch wore off, we had to work harder to maintain our presence. Our thoughts on passive racism and the lack of social awareness possessed by St. Thomas students needed to be shared beyond our internal meetings. Todd often consulted us in our search for ways to broadcast our messages. An avid believer in the power of Black literature, Todd approached the SDIS office about allowing students the opportunity to perform in a spoken word competition as part of their Black History Month programming. The e-board saw the opportunity and made BESA co-sponsors of St. Thomas' first ever slam poetry competition.

"Say what you want to say. This is the opportunity for you to speak up without being censored." Between Todd's encouragement and the colorful anti-establishment rants of SDIS boss Laura, BESA recruited sixteen performers for the slam. Many were BESA members loaded with pent-up frustration and stanzas ready to unleash into the crowd.

"The university done let a *real* nigga in."

James put his right middle finger up while going on about how blessed St. Thomas was to have self-aware Black students grace it. Between furtive glances that read, "Did he really say that?" and "Oh shit, my nigga!" James' poem was one of many untamed performances of the night. A passionate Hmong girl named Kaja went off about White beauty standards, and had another piece about how "Minnesota Nice" fed into passive racism. Selena, a deceptively innocent-looking Mexican-American student and fellow *Strive!* scholar, took every shot at St. Thomas' administration she could: hypocrisy in the school's Catholic tradition, inflated praise of scholarship donors who viewed students of color as high-priced tokens, and overspending on useless campus accessories like an outdoor fountain and swivel chairs were among the topics. Selena left no stone unturned.

Not a single performer held back. Their angst was contagious, giving the room an electricity I never felt on campus before. Staff and students at St. Thomas never said what they truly wanted to say without padding their messages with pleasantries. Compared to the daily experience of awkwardly tense emails and forced smiles, the performances at the slam contest ~~rocked~~ damn near capsized the boat.

SDIS staff and Todd prepared for the administrative backlash. A day went by, then another, and another...but none came. It was a miracle. The White students and staff that came to the event were completely sold on the critical, political vibe many of the performers brought. In finding their own freedom to express frustration, the students of the slam contest opened the eyes of people in positions to solve the very issues addressed in the night's poetry.

The poetry slam was an exciting platform for students who had some shit to say about the campus climate. BESA remained connected to it in following years, but SDIS significantly grew the event's popularity. Other students of color, and even a few White students, began competing in the annual contest. BESA was all for it, but the branding of the event wasn't ours to control anymore. It was all good though, because another huge event during the year of the club's revival left no debate as to what BESA's trademark was going to be.

Traditionally, clubs hosted an annual marquee event that represented the club's mission. These events were crucial to the success of underrepresented racial and cultural clubs. The African student club had African Night, The Hmong student club had Hmong New Year, and so on. Ebony Mic Night was the highlight of past BESA programs, but we needed a new tradition. If BESA was going to pop out again, it had to be something fresh.

We wanted to preserve the tradition of stage performance, but ditch the open mic format. BESA was about giving all types of Black people a platform, so it made sense to invite all types of performers. We wanted beautiful singers, goofy rappers, social activist poets, eccentric dancers and more to share the limelight. A broadly entertaining variety show that stayed true to BESA's harmonious balance of fun-loving and social change-making. Enter, Showtime at the Anderson.

I just landed in ASCeeeee.
The name is Abeye C my color's money greeeen.
That's why I'm the BESA treasurer, yeah I keep that
money cleeean.
I stay fresh to death, I'm such a sight to seeee.

Abeye's goofy ass couldn't hold back a smile as he rapped over the instrumental of "FuckwitmeyouknowIgotit." He was kicking off Showtime at the Anderson, a fun play on Harlem's legendary Black talent showcase *Showtime at the Apollo*. The establishment of

Showtime as BESA's marquee event was the highlight of the club's first semester back.

It was December. A surprisingly large crowd came through Scooter's, an on-campus restaurant in ASC, to see if the fledgling BESA ended the semester with a bang. The only thing easing the anxious crowd before the show was the guarantee of pork ribs, mac and cheese, and cornbread for dinner. Despite our preparedness, the BESA e-board was also anxious. Gin straight from the bottle in James' car was how Abeye, James and I calmed the jitters before we got the show started.

The quick growth of BESA's network was on full display at the Showtime premiere. African, Asian, and Latino members of other multicultural clubs mingled with BESA members in the audience. Students from our sister clubs also had a presence in the show's lineup of acts for the night. White students sat in small clusters all around Scooter's with anxious anticipation.

Between President Mulligan's presence, the increasing visibility of BESA's leaders on campus, and the BLM movement going mainstream, BESA became more than just the Black club. It became a club for anyone who identified with the new age fight for racial equity. Trayvon Martin's death was a fresh memory. Both Eric Garner and Mike Brown left our world only several months prior to BESA's relaunch. BESA became a place for students, faculty and staff at St. Thomas to process the madness of the United States' current social climate. These distraught St. Thomas community members rallied around the club since it was the only campus organization aside from SDIS addressing such issues.

It was cool to see other students of color and St. Thomas faculty and staff feel a sense of obligation to support BESA. It's why performers of so many different backgrounds wanted in on our events. It's why our general meetings started looking like a small-scale United Nations. BESA's reemergence was a rallying cry for students of color, and the occasional White student who wanted to make a difference. It was surprising to see how quickly people on the lethargic campus responded when we took initiative.

We couldn't afford to disappoint with our Showtime premiere. BESA's first semester back needed to end with an exclamation point. Gladly, our supporters stepped up to make Showtime at the Anderson *pop*. People came out of the woodwork with talent we never knew existed on campus. A Black sister-brother duo, a singer and a pianist, blessed us with beautiful covers of soul and R&B classics. A nappy, light-skinned guy who played soccer for the school rapped his ass off and announced his recently released EP. Even Abeye and I got in on the action, surprising people with a joint stand-up comedy routine. The nervous energy Abeye, James and I had before the show became a buzz of pride at the event's success.

The high of a job well done followed us to a post-game party bus, something we thought would be a cool little affair with a couple dozen folks that frequented BESA's meetings and events. Eh, not quite.

As James and I collected entrance fees from familiar faces, the occasional strangers would roll up, hand us their ten dollars, and climb into the bus. More surprising than how quickly news got around about our party bus was the number of White students that wanted to party with us. They wore looks of nervous excitement, the kind you have when you make it to a huge function you weren't actually invited to. Amazingly, a BESA-related event was one of those huge functions that night. For once, White St. Thomas students came to *us* for the turn-up.

"Yo, this bus is *packed.* I didn't think this many people would be standing up." James was borderline concerned since the bus we rented was on the lower end of the seating range. *Not a bad problem to have,* I thought to myself with a smirk.

As we looked back at the bus quickly reaching capacity, people kept coming. James and I shook our heads in incredulity every time a new guest handed their crusty $10 bill and started creeping through the sea of people. We were feeling surprised and overwhelmed, but above all, we were feeling *ourselves.*

"How much did we make?" I asked James.

"Six hundred."

"We made a *profit* off this shit? Also, there's sixty people on this bus??" Aside from maybe being a safety hazard, I was overjoyed. For a group of boys making $9.50 an hour at on-campus jobs, our $150 profit margin was some ballin' ass shit. We tipped the driver to buy out his no-weed policy, then we hit the road.

It's one thing to have the clout to make money off of a dope party. It's another to have earned it off the strength of work that made a difference. Even if St. Thomas was a small, insulated world, BESA's programs and presence as an organized group did a lot for that world. The night of Showtime's premiere was a celebration acknowledging that fact.

The camaraderie felt during my time at BESA has yet to be matched in my life. I finally had a squad, a strong one. We pulled people along for the ride too, including the unfortunate star of the night, Tevin.

Tev was the loyal big dude any complete clique had to have. Seeing that most of our group consisted of 5'7" guys who talked a lot of shit, Tevin's stature and mild-mannered demeanor was always a blessing. He was an old friend of James' who took a break from school after two years at a college in North Dakota. His time was filled with work, weed, and loan debt, a lifestyle that can suck you dry. But whenever Tevin accompanied James to hang around campus, Tevin saw a sanctuary: shiny buildings, good food, pretty women getting their degrees, and fellow Black folks thriving.

Attending BESA events and mingling with club members was very encouraging to Tevin. He even mentioned the possibility of him continuing his studies at St. Thomas. James and I urged him not to do it just for the sake of following a few friends. *He doesn't even know the half of it*, we thought to ourselves. We used to think Tevin's optimistic view of St. Thomas was naïve, but I figured he couldn't have seen much better in North Dakota. In hindsight, his appreciation for what we had at St. Thomas meant a lot about our work with BESA. We convinced a young working class Black adult he could succeed at this rich White Catholic university and genuinely enjoy his time there. Tevin's perspective made us grateful for our time at St. Thomas and proud of the presence we were creating through BESA.

Tev was excited to kick it at St. Thomas even when it was something as mundane as lunch. You could imagine how geeked he was after the Showtime premiere wrapped up. He rolled with us to the party bus with his signature big-ass Bombay bottle in a backpack. As calm as he was, Tevin's insistence on getting himself and his best friends drunk was strong. I've seen his sturdy six-foot frame slumped more often than most of my other friends, which said something about how much alcohol he was throwing back.

Tevin was grown, so of course we weren't paying attention to him as we rode around the city twisted and loose. Everyone was faded, girls twerked, and mild haters sung our praises. Just like the e-board wanted, BESA was ending the semester with an exclamation point. Despite the hot, high-speed commotion of that party bus ride, it felt serene. This was the perfect conclusion to our latest chapter at St. Thomas, and nothing could take us out of our zone...

"HE'S NOT BREATHING. HE'S NOT BREATHING."

Mariela, a Mexican-American sophomore, ran up to James in a panic. His plans of bringing a Black girl named Monica home were dashed as she hopped off of his lap in savior mode. James whipped his head to the right and rushed to the back of the bus. I got there shortly after he did, just in time to see Monica slapping the face of an unresponsive Tevin, pleading with him to say something. He was sprawled across the long bus seat with virtually no control over his movement, lifeless save for his slowed pulse and breathing.

James urgently told the driver to turn around and drop the party off outside of St. Thomas' apartments. The bus was too crowded for everyone to get the message right away. As we approached St. Thomas and people started asking questions, we had to issue a short notice warning that underage drinkers had to dip as soon as they exited the bus.

We called an ambulance over to campus to meet us when we got there. It pulled up soon after we did. The bus driver let the horses out of the stable and madness ensued.

"Wait, what's happening?" "Why are we stopping?" The confusion of our distraught party attendees fell on our deaf, panicked ears.

"Get the fuck off the bus!"

People hurriedly walked to their cars, some ran, some got rounded up by a couple of Public Safety officers who happened to be perched in a nearby truck. The son of a university staff member ran in circles trying to evade an officer before stumbling into drunken disappointment.

The back of the bus had to be opened to transport Tevin into the ambulance. We then hopped out and into James' car, the same whip in which Abeye, James, and I downed liquor and hoped for the best earlier that night. Monica, Briana, our friend Hamza and I piled into James' Infiniti coupe and dipped to Regions Hospital.

An uneasy thirty-minute episode in the waiting room killed our buzz. Not that we cared, we just needed to know Tevin was good. Once he was settled in, James and Hamza went to visit. Tevin was knocked out, but stable. Relief washed over us. We could finally call it a night.

James, Hamza and I had time to reflect after dropping Briana and Monica off in the wee morning hours. We all looked at each other and laughed. *Damn*, we said to ourselves. Some random Black kids formerly best known for loitering in the student center were now popular on-campus leaders. The same random Black kids also threw a party on wheels too lit for its own good. We knew we'd come back that Monday to praise from faculty and staff for our programming. We also knew we gave students a hell of a lot to gossip about. Regardless, we gave St. Thomas something refreshing and memorable that night. BESA was here to stay.

Our solidification as active members of the St. Thomas community took more than one big moment. It was a culmination of efforts both big and small. But BESA was the platform on which it all happened. Years later, BESA continues to be that platform for the Black boys and girls that followed in our footsteps. It's even bigger now, with triple-digit membership and way classier events like a formal soul food dinner and a year-end gala. But Showtime lives on, along with the colorful, ambitious spirit that brought BESA back in the first place.

14

SDIS, Part 1

•••

The name of the Student Diversity and Inclusion Services department said a lot about how the University of St. Thomas understood diversity and inclusion. With four overworked staff members, SDIS was tasked with providing support and programming for *any* student, staff, or faculty member who needed help dealing with St. Thomas' status quo. Aside from Disability Resources and a small, loose group that made up the Queer Straight Alliance, SDIS was the only support hub offered by the university for students struggling to find their place on campus.

Black students, Muslim students, first-gen Americans, low-income students, and undocumented students—basically non-White folk from the city—all frequented this office. International students knowledgeable or curious about U.S. race, class, and gender issues made their way over from the neighboring International Student Services (ISS) office to get active. Both of these offices full of colorful people were tucked away in the corner of the ASC's 2nd floor. Whereas students in ISS were adapting to the United States and meeting other internationals, SDIS was on the frontlines of social justice combat at the university.

Okay, maybe not "combat," but it depended on your background. The more racism you experienced or witnessed before college, the less bothered you were by forms of it on campus. Ask James if 'nigger' spray-painted in a dorm would have kept him from going to class. Ask Johnny if a White person assuming he was a scholarship athlete kept him from graduating. To us, that shit could not compete with the racial housing segregation we woke up to daily. It couldn't compete with black and brown classmates receiving unfair suspensions weekly throughout grade school. It couldn't compete with racial profiling by a cop on an innocent drive home.

If racism and racial identity were relatively new things to you as a person of color, you were liable to have an identity crisis at St. Thomas. At the very least, you'd get smacked with several "aha" moments. More realistically, several "Well *fuck*" moments. It's one thing to know you don't look like a White person. But suddenly realizing the world treated you differently because of your hair texture or skin color could take you from oblivious to hyper-aware of race quickly.

Students with an earlier awareness of race relations found it easier to disregard the annoyances of oblivious White students and administrators. I wasn't bulletproof, but my day wouldn't be ruined by a comment like, "Wow, you're so articulate!" *Ah, yes,* I'd reply in my head. *I'm Black, I speak well. Niggas read and write these days. The world is leaving you behind. What's for lunch?* But to students whose awareness of race came later in life, sensitivity to any apparent racial offense was heightened. People shifted on this spectrum as their racial perspectives changed, but rarely did they remain ambivalent.

Even the students of color most immune to racial slights couldn't always face St. Thomas head on. Most non-White students dissatisfied with the campus climate just kept their heads down until graduation. *This isn't the real world,* we'd say to ourselves. *These people are strange, even for White folks. Not gonna transfer and fuck my credits up, so a couple more years and we're out this bitch.* It wasn't uncommon to ask a Black or Latino student about an on-campus event and get a response like, "Bruh, I just go to class and leave." Any four-year college or university worth its salt at least tried to look like they were invested in keeping their ~~sacred jewels of diversity~~ students of color happy. At St. Thomas, that job was left to the SDIS office.

Prior to my employment at SDIS, the office wasn't much of a hub for student social life. Unless there was a specific reason like discount Timberwolves tickets or registry to the annual Diversity Gala, my friends of color did not go there. I never thought the quiet office hiding in the corner of ASC's second floor would soon become the go-to spot for students of color trying to figure out their new surroundings. I never thought I'd see White social justice "warriors" on campus compelled to be in a space full of black and brown folks. It was hard to imagine the shitstorm of racial equity battles across the nation hitting little old St. Thomas. But it did, and SDIS was going to be the center of it.

Two years prior to me working there, SDIS was adjusting to a staff overhaul. Along with new employees, its location moved from the centralized Murray-Herrick building to a hidden corner of the new student center. Even when students found the office, there wasn't much to stay for. But that changed once their student interns became more visible on-campus leaders.

SDIS was intentional about building relationships with multicultural clubs. Those club members were the students who benefitted the most from SDIS services. The office helped its case by hiring James Thomas our junior year, which brought many of our BESA friends to the office. This is how we connected with Yaia, a delightfully quirky Hmong girl in her third year working at SDIS. She was on the Hmong United Student Association (HUSA) e-board, and also worked at Off-Campus Student Services (OCSS), a hub for many Latino, Hmong and Somali commuter students.

Between BESA's reemergence and Yaia's familiarity with other clubs and ethnic groups on campus, SDIS now had two recognizable student faces as attractions. I was one of those students pulled in by James and Yaia. As I started to get comfortable hanging around the office, I got pulled even further into the SDIS web one day in the fall.

"Hey, are you good with social media?"

"Uh, yeah."

"Want a job?"

"...Sure."

A friendly recommendation from an assistant at the Grants and Research Office convinced Natasha, SDIS' education program director, to hire me as a social media intern on the spot. I started working in the office the second semester of my junior year. Now with two of BESA's leaders in the office, Black students never stopped coming. This also meant more Black students were introduced to Yaia and her network as well. The lax work environment placed an emphasis on building relationships, and we were doing just that. This encouraged more of our friends to visit the office for guidance, or simply for a good time. Much like BESA's come up, it didn't take long for others to rally around SDIS.

The office became a center for dozens of students and faculty who supported multicultural clubs, cared about racial justice, and simply wanted to be around people who cared about the same things. Many of the newcomers were first or second year students looking for a community. The simplest things became important tools in making SDIS an on-campus home. Among the memorable items was a seven-foot long foam bean bag couch that lured people into siesta. There was also a Nerf basketball hoop we taped to a wall and balled on every day, as well as a futon and a fridge full of free food—leftovers from multicultural club meetings—in the storage room. It soon became routine to see a small group of ravenous not-quite-grown boys picking through a container of chicken wings from the latest club meeting.

Sometimes the office looked more like a high school study hall than a work space, but it was for the best. Getting college students involved on campus was hard when they weren't having fun. Between the new, highly visible student interns and the playful attractions, SDIS became the source of fun and support for many students of color on campus. My fellow interns and I brought new life to the office, but the real backbone of SDIS was the underappreciated staff.

Gretchen, the office coordinator of over ten years was the first person you saw when walking in the office. Always smiling, she kept students informed of upcoming events, filled the office candy basket, and kept the other three team members on point. Chris was the retention director, a laidback '08 graduate of St. Thomas. As the leader of a popular summer bridge program for incoming freshmen, Chris was the first staff member many of my peers got to know at St. Thomas. He was cool with just about everyone, his relatability boosted by his youth. His professionalism never slipped, but he was every bit the homie.

Then there was Natasha, a recent graduate of a student affairs Master's program at St. Thomas. Natasha was a short, sweet, biracial (Black and White) woman who played therapist as much as she did her actual job being the education program director. Seeing a student waltz into her office with their feelings and emerge an hour later with a smile and leftover tears was a common sight. Finally, Laura, the head of the office. A fierce Colombian-American who made no secret of her desire to flip the institution on its head. She wore her heart on her sleeve, cursed under her breath, and gave students daily tips on how to finesse the school's resources. Latinx or not, students that saw her frequently enough were "mijo/mija" to her.

Staff outside of the office didn't think twice about how burdened SDIS was. They expected this group of four to serve and support every demographic outside of White, straight, and Catholic, then figure out a way to involve White, straight, Catholic people to avoid criticism for being exclusionary. Everyone in SDIS worked fifty or more hours a week, and constantly dealt with the stress of identity politics.

It was in every facet of their jobs. Whether they were working with students, faculty, staff, or off-campus partners, the success of SDIS staff relied on how well they understood race, gender, sexuality, and class dynamics in every interaction. Identity politics consumed all of them, but their experiences helped students understand how a university worked. Things like the motivations behind donor scholarships[1], or the language used on the school website to discuss diversity became clearer through many candid conversations held in that office. SDIS was a sociocultural plug helping us move smarter on campus.

There were a number of faculty and staff committed to supporting students of color, but the four good people at SDIS were the only ones who dealt with all aspects of student life on a daily basis. If you were fucking up in school, uncomfortable on campus, or just didn't know where to go for things, SDIS had answers. The office was unconditionally supportive, pretty much family on campus. The family grew my senior year when four good friends were coincidentally hired as the office interns. Along with Yaia and I came Abeye's jolly self and Cory, a third year student and BESA member.

Abeye and Cory were still on BESA's e-board, and the club was even more lit than it was last year. The leadership now consisted mostly of second and third year Black women, including Faith, Cory's girlfriend. Between last year's success, younger leaders, gender parity, and the fledgling power couple, dozens of fresh-faced

Black and African students flocked to BESA. Along with Yaia's consistent recruitment of OCSS and HUSA students, SDIS became dumb popular. Much like BESA became *the* club last year, SDIS became *the* spot for all these students.

The racial and cultural diversity SDIS attracted was wild. Seeing the variety of folks in the office was hard to believe after experiencing St. Thomas for years prior. There were Ethiopian-American kids, African internationals, Hmong-Americans, Nigerian-Americans, more Nigerians (a *surplus*, Nigerians are everywhere I swear). I never thought I'd see the Fouas and Sais of the world interact with Mohameds and Adebolas at St. Thomas. It was like those cramped, chaotic hallways of Central High School again. The real world was finally on campus.

SDIS was active in their support for the multicultural clubs, co-sponsoring events, strategizing, and marketing for them. A serious push for a more inclusive campus was happening in this compact web of people, and SDIS was the only school department really involved. Given the office's place in the development of our de facto cross-cultural coalition, it was no surprise that our protest of the university began there.

Clubs like BESA and HUSA were used to frustrating treatment from the university. For instance, Dining Services restricted off-campus catering and insisted on making (fucking up) culturally specific foods for events. Even before getting to that step, multicultural clubs often dealt with unnecessary pushback on event funding requests. But a line was crossed when the Undergraduate Student Government (USG) sent out fall semester budgets my senior year.

Typically, clubs got between fifty to one-hundred percent of their requested budgets. You could imagine the surprise of BESA, the African Nations Student Association (ANSA), Globally Minded Student Association (GMSA), and HUSA when they received either no money, or a third of what they asked for at best.

SDIS hosted a small forum three days later to discuss rising racial tension on campuses across the nation. Talking points included news of Mizzou's racist death threats—the ones that inspired Concerned Student 1950—and the bullshit budgets St. Thomas' multicultural clubs received. Along with a couple dozen faithful SDIS constituents, many of the office's infrequent patrons, committed faculty, and a bunch of White students from the Social Justice and Peace club showed up. Even stiff-ass, out-of-touch Provost Bob Pear came through. The space reached capacity, something that never happened for SDIS' weekly discussions.

The movements of Mizzou, Yale, and dozens of other student bodies ripping racism out of their school's roots swept the nation that year. Laura's rebellious self wanted us to ride the revolutionary wave. We seemed like a united front, an inspired group of underrepresented students backed by SDIS. But we never thought we'd become our own opposition. With so many examples of well-organized racial equity movements at college campuses across the country, ours was a straight-up disaster.

15

SDIS, Part 2

•••

"There are people in this room who were talking shit about me and SDIS! They don't even understand what they've done for us!

"We want to be involved, but we didn't even know about the document or where it was at! We've been left out!"

"I just think that you've been shoving this movement down our throats."

"WE'VE ONLY DONE THESE THINGS TO HELP YOU. SO UNGRATEFUL."

SDIS' relationship with students hit a low point that winter. A series of chaotic events saw the office's years of hard work building trust and familiarity with students of color dissipate in a week.

After the forum where we vented about the club budgets, SDIS helped multicultural club leaders and members plan a sit-in protest at the next USG meeting. The meetings were hosted on Sundays and were generally quiet, internal affairs. But with forty multicultural club members and leaders posted up in the room, business as usual was disrupted. That Sunday evening was time to stop letting shit slide.

The protest was strange. We had to wait silently in the corner for twenty minutes before USG reached the agenda item concerning multicultural club budgets. That's when we rose from our seats and held our signs up, mostly messages about the lack of regard St. Thomas showed for its multicultural clubs and students. We had the floor to speak, and many of the younger protesters took a minute or two to condemn USG for their poor treatment of the clubs. The USG members who responded offered surface-level condolences and danced around the issue with formalities. Kaja, Yaia's fiery younger sister, did not feel like playing along that night.

"You have to meet us where we're at, we can't keep coming to you telling you how to help us," explained a young freshman girl. The idea that White student leaders had to actually *try* along with us to make racial equity happen didn't seem to register.

"I feel bad about the mistakes I made with the budget," said the USG finance guy. "Let me know how to help you all! My office hours are 2 p.m. to 4 p.m. and y—"

"WE DON'T CARE ABOUT HOW YOU FEEL. WHAT ARE YOU ACTUALLY GOING TO DO TO FIX THIS?"

Everyone in the room jumped up a bit. All of the protesters turned and looked like, "Damn, Kaja!" Her outburst and subsequent rant got us going. It encouraged several more students to follow up with their own criticisms of USG's apathy. Demands for transparency and intentional collaboration were beaten into their heads. We didn't know if any of this would result in actual change, but at least we left USG shook.

The university had a history of sweeping controversy under the rug. With our protest and Kaja's eruption, it became impossible to do so. Building off this momentum, we finally gave a name to our movement: SOCCOS—Students of Color: Claim Our Seats (rolls right off the tongue, eh?). We then communicated with President Mulligan to hold an event where protesters and affiliated folks could voice their concerns and call for specific action. President Mulligan announced an "open forum" event despite our request for a closed session between the protest leaders and the President. Given recent backlash from St. Thomas students on Facebook in response to the protest, some of us didn't agree with having people who didn't sympathize with the protesters there to watch them in a vulnerable moment.

We couldn't get that to happen, so we went on with it. Even if some random White students wanted to see what all the commotion was about, I saw the increased exposure as a positive. Those students, along with President Mulligan and Provost Pear, had to come face-to-face with our dissatisfied community. Along with our verbal criticism came a thorough document of recommendations for a more racially equitable campus. Raymond, a level-headed Cameroonian student, spearheaded the writing of the document along with Yaia, an SDIS grad student assistant and I just two days prior. We proudly delivered it to President Mulligan during the open forum.

Our heated group of protesters had a lot going for it that week: receipts of USG's fuckery, a concrete list of requests for the administration, and the attention of both the President and Provost. For once, frustrated students of color had a chance to have a lasting impact on St. Thomas' culture. Surely we wouldn't implode when things were going so well, would we?

Shakes head, sighs Young people.

One frustrating part about the open session, as well as the entire movement, was the battle over how the movement best served our interests. Some of us closely tied to SDIS, myself included, wanted to urgently push short-term reform ideas before graduation. Our primary focus was the recommendations document. Some people wanted to use the movement as a personal soapbox, saving their rants and tears about racism for SOCCOS meetings, including the open session. Those who saw the necessity of both behaviors got confused trying to find a compromise.

The small band of us pushing the recommendations—soon dubbed "The Document"—didn't want President Mulligan to see us sobbing. We didn't want to be pitied. As seniors ready to graduate, and with winter break threatening our momentum, we wanted to quickly lay groundwork for younger SOCCOS members to build from. With some guidance from Laura, we wasted no time contacting President Mulligan about The Document. This rubbed other SOCCOS members the wrong way.

Not everyone knew what they were actually there to do, but many SOCCOS members were still new to processing issues of race. This protest was the greatest and only chance at activism many of these students had at the time. I didn't blame them for using SOC-COS as a space to express race-related frustration. But after Yaia and Raymond announced our communication with President Mulligan about The Document, much of SOCCOS' frustration was redirected at its leaders.

Dissonance in our goals turned SOCCOS' focus inward. Instead of pressuring President Mulligan, we grilled each other. Behind each other's backs, fellow protesters criticized others for being overinvolved or not involved enough. The childish tension played out on the SOCCOS Facebook page in debates about who got to do and say certain things. Students started suggesting role titles, committees, and other ways to denote everyone's authority. Apparently, the fight with St. Thomas for seats at the table wasn't the more important power struggle.

We didn't have time for it, but the concerns kept growing. Concerns grew into criticisms of those leading the charge. Most of the disapproval was directed at Yaia and Kaja. *Why are two Asian-American women speaking for all of us? Why do they have such good relationships with SDIS? Why aren't we allowed to be in their positions?* Doubts of the sort grew into exaggerated fears. Students didn't want to go unheard. They also wanted to feel like SDIS cared about all of them equally. Questions about the SOCCOS leadership's lack of transparency and the amount of support they received from SDIS, an office meant for *all* of them, became a divide.

I was livid. Raymond, Abeye, and I found ourselves quickly growing dissatisfied with the direction of the movement. Were we going to respect our unique viewpoints and put something together for the future of this university? Or were we going to undermine each other over who got to say and do whatever for a month-long stint in the campus spotlight? Even if we got past the pettiness, there were too many different groups to account for. ANSA, HUSA, BESA, GMSA, Latinos Unidos, USG members of color, and underrepresented students not affiliated with SOCCOS felt entitled to decide on how SOCCOS should operate. No one was willing to let one or two people speak on behalf of the whole movement.

Neither SOCCOS nor SDIS could make everyone happy. But the fuzzy communication between SOCCOS leaders and constituents didn't warrant the bickering that resulted. The shortsighted feuding dragged all of us down. Beef between a small faction of girls and Yaia and Kaja raged on, while younger members complained about their lack of involvement. The tension led Raymond and Kaja to call a meeting of about thirty people, including Laura, to air out grievances.

That brought us to the calamitous December night of the SOCCOS schism, a low-budget parody of a *Dear White People* scene. People came eager to talk shit about their fellow protesters as well as SDIS, the only university department that looked out for our best interests. An hour and a half of accusations and acrimony, but no answers.

The downside to Kaja's otherwise inspiring passion was how deeply personal this all became to her. Off bat, she shouted the names of people who had slight to strong concern about her and SDIS' role in the movement. This set the tone for the rest of the meeting. While Kaja was getting into it with people trying to root out the dissenters, a freshman boy showed up twenty minutes late, raised his hand, and accused Laura to her face of, "shoving it [the movement] down our throats."

Writing in caps doesn't capture the rage Laura expressed. She saw a student she grew fond of, one of her "mijos," completely trash her in front of a group, including an administrator brought in to mediate the meeting. I was sympathetic to her incensed yelling, but it was a bad look in front of students divided in their opinion of her. Following that up was another freshman boy speaking for younger SOCCOS members about the lack of clarity concerning the plan for The Document. His complaint was interrupted multiple times by the ongoing fuck-SDIS drama.

The entire ordeal was gross, like watching different colored crabs in a bucket. I knew I was one of them, so I stopped scrambling and let myself sink to the bottom. Watching everyone climb and pull each other down was hardly any better than participating in it. I realized we were hopeless either way. We didn't support each other, so St. Thomas didn't support our movement.

Within a month of the protest and The Document's creation, the seniors who helped lead the initial charge fell back. Raymond, Abeye, Yaia, Kaja and I were simply done. Seeing our characters questioned for simply working in SDIS and moving swiftly on behalf of SOCCOS was infuriating. Sure, the organization wasn't perfect. But to think we somehow gained more from being the de facto leaders of this struggle movement was ridiculous. As if I'd put "Led small-scale racial justice battle at super White school" on my résumé and become a Twitter celebrity or something.

Remember what I said about the St. Thomas community allowing space for only a few of us? That only a handful of ambassador-type students outside of mainstream St. Thomas could actually thrive? Well, the sad part is we bought into this mentality too. All of us, the disgruntled students of color trying to leave their mark, wanted to steer this movement to prominence. Instead of breaking the curse and winning together in the long-run, we tore each other up over a couple of make-believe spots of power.

We were supposed to do it for incoming freshmen. For people that would want just one or two more good reasons to keep going when they found it tough at St. Thomas. We were doing it so future students didn't have to bawl their eyes out in front of dozens just to have their struggles recognized. But seeing people mostly driven by the desire to feel important killed the vibe.

There were small victories stemming from the chaos of our movement that actually made me proud. I attended an event a year later where the hallway SDIS was located in was renamed after the first Black student at St. Thomas, Father John Henry Dorsey. Laura and I did some digging and found out about him my senior year. We agreed for me to share our findings as part of Purple Bench, our weekly office discussion about relevant social and cultural issues. Apparently, this guy was the second ever ordained Black priest in the country and was friends with Booker T. Washington[1].

Cory, the tall, gangly, soft-spoken homie, was particularly impressed with the story. Cory and I didn't know what people thought of the recent discovery until Laura started barking at us about innovative ways for St. Thomas to display its commitment to diversity and inclusion. A lot of schools were changing building names and defacing statues of slave-owning forefathers at the time. According to Cory, simply changing the name of the hallway outside of SDIS from "Campus Way" to "Dorsey Way" was a less dramatic but significant step on the otherwise slow-moving St. Thomas campus.

One petition, 250 student signatures and two semesters later, Dorsey Way became official. There was a dedication ceremony, and thorough profiles of both Dorsey and Cory were published in the university's newsletter. It was a happy medium, the long overdue silver lining of SOCCOS' failure. The sprouting of a seed planted in turmoil. Perhaps change required a balance. Patience and impatience. Order and chaos.

Though SOCCOS didn't successfully push its reforms, it influenced the birth of an organization that addressed the same issues. The Diversity Activities Board (DAB), expertly named by Natasha at the peak of the Migos-fueled dance craze, was installed by St. Thomas a semester after I graduated. DAB received a six-figure budget and the responsibility of adding a significant amount of educational programming to the university around topics of diversity and inclusion. DAB's creation directly addressed SOCCOS' concern with St. Thomas students' lack of social awareness, as well as the lack of resources (i.e. space and money) given to support underrepresented students. DAB made SOCCOS worth it, the perfect example of chaos reordering things for the better.

Not all racial justice movements are created equally. The story of SOCCOS wasn't worthy of a HuffPost article like countless other college protests. But even though we didn't get results when and how we wanted them, results came. It wasn't pretty, and there wasn't much to show for it while I was a student, yet the movement was still worth it. The experience with SOCCOS put larger racial justice movements into a greater perspective. Like wow, how did SNCC and the SCLC accomplish all of that in the 1960s? How did BLM become so prominent today without official leaders?

There's no perfect way to fight against large-scale injustice. A small, private Catholic school in Minnesota isn't the largest of opponents, but an uphill battle nonetheless. We were inexperienced, impatient, and disjointed as fuck. Still, we acted, and it was way better than doing nothing.

16

When The Bubble Bursts

•••

On November 23, 2015, Allan "Lance" Scarsella pulled up to a Black Lives Matter protest in North Minneapolis at the city's 4th police precinct. Jamar Clark, an unarmed Black man, was shot dead just eight days prior by an MPD officer. Lance and several of his friends had been hovering around the protests for several days, ridiculing them as they livestreamed the action. Racial slurs poured out behind the facemasks they wore, along with sentences like, "We are locked and loaded. We are going to make the fire rise."

In all their sinister eagerness, the livestream video circulated online and quickly caught the attention of local BLM protest organizers. So when Lance and company walked up to the protest on the 23rd, they were quickly met with protesters demanding them to remove their masks. Refusing to do so, the small group of masked men walked one block down until the protesters fell back. It would have been left at that if the eerie troublemakers didn't feel so bold that day.

As they walked away, a group of seven BLM protesters overheard the masked gang shout 'niggers'. The protesters went back to the marauding men to confront their open racism. With his recklessness up, and angry Black people running toward him as the ultimate excuse, Lance opened fire. He emptied his pistol on the group of seven protesters who had confronted him and his terrorist associates. Five were hit. The day after, local news reported no one had died from the wounds suffered from the shooting. While that was a blessing, the Lance Scarsella story got uglier.

It was revealed that one year before the shooting, Lance posted an image of a flag linked to the Confederacy on his Facebook profile. Racist text messages sent by him weeks before the attack were also uncovered. Texts included a request to attend target practice with a friend, "for when we have to shoot black guys." Another text suggested, "smelly brown people" should kill themselves. During his trial, it was also discovered he had texted a Burnsville police officer, a friend of his, with hints at his plan to shoot up the 4th precinct protests days before doing so. The cop soon resigned after giving his revealing testimony, one where he dubbed his racially-charged conversations with Lance as "locker room talk." And the icing on the cake, at least for my friends and I, was the reveal of his alma mater: the University of St. Thomas.

Not only did he graduate from St. Thomas, he walked among my classmates. A Spring 2015 grad, Lance Scarsella strolled by us going to and from class, breakfast, lunch, dinner, and events for *years* prior to this story. In fact, he shared a Biology class with my friend Hamza, a Somali male. Apparently Lance was kind to my friend. They were even friends on Facebook, and the screenshot of Lance's Confederacy-related flag post displayed Hamza's standalone "Like" of the post. Its uncanny resemblance to the national flag of

Somalia, blue with a white star, deceived Hamza. Lance definitely made sure to clarify, though. "This isn't the somalian flag, btw," he commented in response. Lance's use of the inaccurate term "somalian" was annoying, but no reason to believe his now creepy cliffhanger comment was an omen.

The irony of Lance's interaction with Hamza continues to make me chuckle about an otherwise dark memory. Maybe he didn't consider Somali folks to be Black. Maybe his racism was so passive that in the presence of a person he was supposed to hate on principle, he simply knew better than to be a racist asshole. It's funny to think that the act which put him on the map as a racist could have been his first outward expression of racism in front of other Black people.

When it comes down to race relations, Midwestern polity—meaning "Minnesota Nice," which *really* means "White and suburban/rural Minnesota Nice"—makes revelations like this shocking...kinda. If Lance Scarsella was an alum of the University of Louisiana-Lafayette who opened fire at a Baton Rouge BLM protest, I wouldn't be surprised. In fact, a young Klansman-in-training would be what I *expect* out of Louisiana. Their racism is supposed to be loud, Cajun-flavored and in your face. But with so much of Minnesota's race issues being whispered about and swept under the rug, such an explicit example of these problems did carry some shock value.

Many of my friends accused other Minnesotans of passive-aggressiveness all the time. This homebred terrorist attack, however, was passive-AGGRESSIVE in a way we've never seen. It's one thing for a pessimistic St. Thomas student to walk around thinking, "All these motherfuckers are racist." But it's something else entirely to see one of your peers on the front page of the Star Tribune's website looking like the failed Midwestern version of Dylan Roof. It just hit too close to home. At least if you weren't White, that is.

I get it. As aware as I was, I still lived in and benefitted from the bubble St. Thomas created around itself. But only when you let the temporary atmosphere of college numb your feelings about the state of the world do you become the sheltered millennial older critics desperately try to make us all seem. This could be said about social justice "warriors" of all races who preach to the choir nonstop just to be a part of something, then retract the militant anti-White supremacy tweets when they haven't read a trendy story about a slain Black person in a while. But generally speaking, those who buy into the college experience at the expense of detaching from the world are those who can *afford* to.

In the literal sense, yes, the wealthiest among my classmates were pretty easy to identify. So was their aloofness. But the price I'm alluding to wasn't monetary, it was of the heart. The currency was identity. Can you, a person from (a place) who's been identified as (a label) and considers people of (a place or a label) to be close to you, afford to lose your investment in those people? Could you read a story about Latino families in Minneapolis being deported without thinking about a friend? Could you read about the three Muslim students and alum of UNC and NC State killed by a White man over a parking dispute without thinking about your sister? Your neighbor?

When you grow up in the city, you invest more of that currency into others by default, regardless of how impersonal you are when you walk down the street. It's why White folks from Central were so much different from White folks at St. Thomas. When I said Central folks *had* to see us, I meant they *had* to invest in us. The sickness, health, success and failure of Somali kids, hood niggas, quiet Hmong kids, and Mexican boys and girls affected how White people at Central felt about their community. Even if they were awkward and difficult about it, they *had* to care. But in the bubble we called St. Thomas, most White people, which meant most people, did not. They simply did not have to care.

So when news of Lance Scarsella rolled around and the timid address from President Mulligan landed in our inboxes, no one but those closest to me talked about it. The heaviness of the air in SDIS and amongst my friends when discussing the subject immediately dissolved into the sterile atmosphere of campus. Our furrowed brows and frustration seemed out of place. Our concerned vibe seemed to swerve around White students who were in our midst, as if the story was of a distant country that only affected a select few. This wasn't true in terms of geography, but it became clear that community in this case meant more than a shared location.

Within the campus bubble that everyone lived in, our White peers seemed to have their own personal bubbles. They seemed able to remove themselves from their bubbles, proven by the rare wannabe White allies that infrequently showed up to SDIS and BESA programs. But for the most part, they stayed in those bubbles. The strength of their bubbles' ability to repel life's harsh realities came from their distance: distance from the knowledge of our experience, physical evasion of the places we grew up, and distance from their own identities. In an increasingly connected world, many of the students we walked past daily were detached. Detached enough to create a new world, and too detached to understand they were unfairly subjecting others to it.

My friends and I had our bubbles popped that week, and the strength of all the White students' bubbles pissed us off. But the strength of our compassion was truer, a fact we had to hold on to.

17

Ball Is Not Life

•••

One thing I immediately liked about St. Thomas was its sporting culture. Despite being an NCAA Division 3 school, St. Thomas' athletics had a regional reputation they took seriously. The competitive streak wasn't limited to their official student-athletes either. Many students not on a school team played a sport through a club, intramurals, or recreationally. Others were dedicated weightlifters, serial runners, or both. The glimmering new recreation center was almost always accessible to us athletic commoners. It was a haven, especially to a group of young Black kids looking to get away from the daily stress of campus life.

Complaints about St. Thomas never followed my friends and I into the gym. We were too busy trying to bust each other's asses on the basketball court. No, we weren't training to go legit. Most of us didn't even bother with intramurals until the last half of our college careers. But as Black city boys, young men co-parented by neighborhood rec centers, basketball was *the* sport to play. It wasn't about making your name off of sports. Whether you were all-state or stopped playing organized sports after 12U, it didn't matter. Being able to hoop was more than that. It was socialization. It was education.

Hooping is like learning cursive in the third grade: something an adult rarely has to use, but needs to know so as not to look dumb as fuck when put on the spot. If you, a Black boy in the city, grew up unable to do something as simple as a crossover dribble, or even a chest pass, niggas clowned the fuck out of you. If you hung around Black kids that did not study 24/7 or dedicate their lives to a career path—pretty much all of us as teens—you needed to learn basketball for the benefit of your self-esteem. Forget hoop dreams, the court was a coming-of-age test.

This is what made Darrell's one and only showing on the court hysterical. A track athlete with a freakish understanding of sports physiology, Darrell seemed competent in most sports. We knew he had a proven track record as a sprinter, mid-distance runner, football player, and weightlifter. But what we *didn't* know was that he wasn't nearly as experienced of a hooper as he claimed.

For all his quirkiness and intellectualism, Darrell grew up in the hood. I'm sure he had to convince people he could ball every so often. Perhaps he was decent in his youth before deciding to focus on other things. But the day he came to hoop during the fall semester of our sophomore year, Darrell was *trash*. His shot was whack. His handles were loose like old doorknob screws. Darrell had us laughing every time he touched the ball.

The icing on the cake was his notorious "euro step," a skill he insisted on bragging about. He even went so far as to curse those who travelled—took more than two steps without dribbling, for my non-hoopers—under the guise of a euro-step. As he charged into the lane, Darrell waved the ball back and forth in the air with two hands and took four enormous steps on his way to the basket. We were on the ground dying for air before he got his shot off, all of us shouting, "Bro, that's a travel!" while cracking up[1].

"Fam, that was a euro step!" Darrell rebuked in his energized tenor voice. He was every bit the homie, but we showed him no mercy. Like any good group of Black male friends would, we let him down hard on that one. With his only point of hooping pride shot, Darrell took the loss and walked off the court.

Darrell's performance that day was comedy, but I was no stranger to unorthodox styles of basketball. St. Paul and Minneapolis hosted a huge intercultural pool of hoopers which made for many different player types. As an Ethiopian kid held back in my hooping education by my time in South Dakota, I was comforted seeing other racial and ethnic groups included in the "Ball is life" narrative. I grew up watching Hmong kids pull up to courts squaded up, surviving on floaters and midrange shooting. Somali dudes, and even the occasional hijabi, played basketball with recklessness and zeal. White boys were rarely the most creative, but their conservative play and consistent jumpshots were refreshing in a sea of folks who all thought they could take over a game singlehandedly.

You'd never think you could understand someone based on how they tried to put a leather ball in a basket. But that's what happens when you have a bunch of people of different backgrounds trying to accomplish the same thing. Given the diversity of styles and the lack of truly dominant players, anyone on courts across the Twin Cities could shine in any given pickup game.

Much like the gyms of LA Fitness or the rec center by my old high school, the guys I hooped with at St. Thomas were a strange assortment. My hand-eye coordination and lack of height led me to develop skills like my notoriously out of reach hook shot. Hamza scrapped for messy buckets and played way-too-physical defense—a hack, in other words. Trokon was shifty, adept at stealing the ball and holding onto it by dribbling inches off the ground. Johnny's go-to move was to sprint to his right all the way to the hoop, usually with a knee or foot up for anyone trying to defend him. Loath to running, Abeye planted himself on the three-point line and prayed for open shots, getting hot when we least expected it.

We weren't the only ones with niche hooping abilities that came out to play on campus. White boys, offseason football players, and lightskinned Black suburbanites took hooping as seriously as we did. Despite the occasional arguments that inevitably happen when Black folk play pickup, basketball was the simplest part of our social experience at St. Thomas. Our motley crew of hoopers played almost daily during my sophomore year. We couldn't get enough. Our coursework hadn't overwhelmed us yet, we had no idea how to apply ourselves outside of class, and we all lived on campus. For all of us, it was the last great opportunity to regularly play basketball with friends before adulthood gave us more important things to do.

It was an atmosphere where James Thomas felt comfortable toying with the idea of trying out for the school team. It was an atmosphere where we could all chase individual glory, win, and get buckets to brag about for a lifetime. We also made sure to not take it so seriously, sometimes showing up to the gym drunk or high for the hell of it. Memories like that, or losing to Johnny one-on-one after I called his jumpshot garbage, were the types of stories that gave us ownership of our St. Thomas experience. Not all of our great moments of camaraderie had to be in response to a racist incident or some shared frustration to mean something. Basketball was a simple joy in an otherwise complicated college journey.

With all that time and all of those resources, college briefly allowed us to pretend ball was life. We all knew it wasn't. We were in college for degrees, not the NBA draft. Our life was going to consist of much more than parties and basketball the closer we got to graduation, but that's why our hooping routine was such a blessing. It was a fun getaway, away from the draining pressures of fitting into an institution that wasn't built for us. It was something to bond over other than the color of our skin.

Basketball was socialization. Basketball was education. As I fixated on the game, I couldn't help but get to know the people I was playing it with. White boys, football players, and lightskinned dudes became familiar faces. My group of go-to hoopers picked up on the bits and pieces of life that followed each of us to the gym and reappeared on the way out. We learned more about each other. We processed the events of a day together before hitting the court, and made plans to link up again once we finished. It connected us in an easygoing way that student clubs, classes and parties couldn't. Ball was not life, but it was a big part of making life at St. Thomas better.

18

Facing a Bottle of Henny

•••

It was Abeye's 23rd birthday. Eighteen months of patience gave him an impressive set of dreadlocks that lifted his aesthetic, and his confidence, way past his buzz cut days. He was an admissions counselor at St. Thomas now, an unthinkable reality when we first met on campus as freshmen. As a respected alumnus and spokesperson of the school we used to bash, Abeye's cheery brown face was the first face thousands of teenagers that year saw in connection to St. Thomas. Abeye's genuine delight in sticking around encouraged his fellow Black graduates to own St. Thomas as their alma mater rather than neglect the association. Abeye's presence also became popular among current students of color, showing them that they, too, could grow and have fun there.

Almost a year removed from being college students, Abeye and I were not quite done with the turn-up at St. Thomas. Several younger peers, including Cory, agreed to host Abeye's birthday night pregame at their on-campus apartment. Ten minutes in the nostalgic setting, and I found myself in awe at how quickly things were changing on campus. *Where the fuck did y'all come from?!* I exclaimed to myself as I gawked at the swarm of new black and brown students on my walk to the apartment. Their energy left a greater impression on me than their numbers, youthful heads of kinky curls and dreads freely buzzing around as if they were at an HBCU. One of Cory's roommates told me half of the orientation leaders the previous summer were of color. Many of the leaders' names I recognized as wide-eyed freshmen who used to tiptoe into BESA meetings a year ago.

I looked at Abeye and remembered how content he was hanging out with White boys who didn't respect him, and White girls who kept him around as entertainment. He wasn't much of a sucker anymore, a young man with enough self-respect to not drool over a cute face, and enough confidence to roast someone audacious enough to say, "I don't *really* see you as Black." His dreads weren't playthings for girls at the bar or his coworkers to be superficially obsessed about. They were a unique expression of his Black self in blank spaces, tied and twisted in new ways each month as if to say, "Keep up," to White peers who tried and failed to label him. St. Thomas showed Abeye he didn't have the sauce, but it also encouraged him to get some. Abeye finally stopped letting people decide who he was.

In my eyes, Abeye was the embodiment of the changes and growth of St. Thomas' Black student community over the last five years: still a bit awkward and shy at times, but clearly starting to come into its (his) own. To match his loud laugh and the proud statement of his hair, Abeye showed up to his party in brand new Jordan sneakers, red and Black 13s. His eagerness was childlike, a huge step from being ridiculed by a White sneakerhead for wearing fake Jordan 11s our sophomore year. With the fresh fit and his good friends around him, the birthday boy was ready to put the cherry on top of his rebranded Blackness. Only one of Abeye's requests was left to be fulfilled.

"Ay bruh, gotchu a lil' somethin' for ya birthday."

Lincoln, an old friend of Cory's, came through to share in the festivities. Along with his well wishes, Lincoln presented Abeye with a couple of birthday trophies: two 750 mL offerings of cognac. One was Remy Martin, a drink he bragged, "Will put some hair on ya chest." But the other was the true prize, a staple at Black parties across the country. Something "very special" as stated on the label, the drink of triumph for Black Americans ranging from WWII veterans to today's most popular rappers. The smooth, classy, somewhat overrated brown elixir called Hennessy[1].

Between his Bachelor's degree, new job, and newfound confidence, there were many victories in Abeye's time at St. Thomas to celebrate that night. Completing the obstacle course of racism and isolation on campus deserved the reward of friends and adult beverages. Any bitterness experienced over the years at St. Thomas was now overshadowed by this joyous buzz. Likewise, the bitterness of the forthcoming shots was about to become a heartwarming tipsiness that powered us through the night. Abeye, and everyone celebrating with him, deserved a delicious moment to wash down the challenging taste of St. Thomas. A few seconds of shuddering throat burn wasn't going to keep our boisterous band of brown folk from getting drunk off the brown. Finally, Abeye was ready to face a bottle of Henny.

A Toast (Acknowledgements)

•••

To Jadea Washington and Josh Plattner for volunteering their time to review and edit a whole damn book. It means so much that your belief in me as a person, let alone a writer, was enough to bring you both on board. Jadea, your constant challenges to my perspective took this piece from a super long journal entry to a real-deal memoir. Go get you that Master's degree! Josh, your considerate guidance assured me of my voice's value and gently pushed my stories in the right direction. Many thanks, and I wish you well in your life's next chapter. To Jadea and Josh *sips*.

To Sunita Dharod for patiently taking my incessant directions and turning them into this book's classy lookin' cover. You've really invested yourself in this book, and you've been nothing but optimistic and driven throughout the creative process. You deserve praise, and a dope ass job as soon as you graduate. To Sunita *sips*.

To Dr. David Todd Lawrence, Dr. Buffy Smith, Chris, Muhdi, James, Johnny, Kaja, Cory, Philipo, Raymond, Gabbie, Darrell, Hamza, Selena, and Tobias for the candid, thoughtful input you gave me in support of the memoir's accuracy and the quality of my reflections. You all joined me in being open, and at times vulnerable, for the sake of the book. Most of you also let me use your actual names, an extra level of sincerity I greatly appreciate. I hope I did you all justice and that you feel good about your contribution to this work. To my interviewees *sips more than last time*.

To Hughbert, Abeye, Matt, Gauthier, Gaelord, Faith, Tevin, and Trokon, the good friends I didn't interview that allowed me to use their real names in association with my memories of them. They must really trust me or something. I could have said some *really* crazy shit. Friendship is such a beautiful thing. To y'all *gulps*.

To Dickie Bhee, the secretive yet wildly uncensored online social criticism blogger that opened my eyes to the reality of self-publishing via a DM conversation on Twitter. Though I've never seen this guy's face, interacting with such a prolific writer gave me the confidence to boldly pursue writing in more serious forms such as this book. There are times when something is unfolding in front of me that I think to myself, "Hmm, I would love to write a piece on this. What would Dickie Bhee call it?" I answer the question, omit the blatantly offensive words, and voila! A night of nostalgia and brown liquor drinking becomes *Facing a Bottle of Henny*. Sooo coool! I gotta do this again. Anyway, thanks Dickie Bhee. To you *gulps*.

Finally, to my mom, my dad, my sister, and my girlfriend. You weren't my editors, graphic designers, or interviewees, but you all gave me the love and support necessary to feel *hiccup* like I could accomplish this work in the first place. All the heart emojis. To my loved ones *realizes his glass is empty, pours more, sips*.

Well, I'm definitelyyyyy lightheaded. Let's keep going! You're probably like, "You ended it so beautifully! Why sabotage yourself by rambling in this outro?" And I'm like, "I know, I know, but I got these thoughts, I can't just let them slide." Besides, outros are the longest parts of some really good projects. Kanye's "Last Call" anyone? J. Cole's "Note to Self"? Drake's "Pound Cake/Paris Morton Music 2"?

I don't know what business I have calling myself a book author. First of all, I'm surprised you stuck with it long enough to even read this. Even at a lean 160ish pages, this shit is waaaaay longer than a Buzzfeed article or a tweet. Not to mention it isn't as automated as your Netflix account or Spotify playlists. You actually flipped the pages and shit (or scrolled through on the e-book version, but that's work too), and processed all these words? I love you. But for real, to have a publication in the form of a book, whatever the content may be about, has now given me a taste of being on the other side of the conversation. The questioned rather than the questioner. At twenty-two years of age, however confident I may be, I still can't act like I have the answers to everything about Blackness, Whiteness, college, social class, intersec—

Yo, cut this man off!

Ay, nobody asked you how you felt about this outro, damn it. You gon' tell me to stop talking in my own book?! You're lucky that's good advice, or else I'd just keep going to irritate you. Like how them politicians filibuster and shit. You know they talk for a day *straight* sometimes?? And it's all just to stall the government as if they don't got some real shit to do like, great, you're not petty at all, my guy. Just go ahead and—aight, aight, I'll stop.

Downs glass, stumbles away from table with a grin, and walks out.

Endnotes

...

Pregame

1. At an on-campus Halloween party my freshman year, I went dressed as Carlton Banks (i.e. sweater, slacks, short flattop, my face) from The Fresh Prince of Bel Air. Didn't know many people two months into college, so I thought the recognizable outfit and my mastery of The Carlton Dance would be great icebreakers. Two-thirds of the people I encountered didn't even know who Carlton Banks was, let alone that I was supposed to look like him. One of my greatest disappointments at St. Thomas.

BMOC

1. PBUH (peace be upon him) is a formality used after a direct mention of the prophet Muhammad (PBUH) out of respect.

Scrubby

1. The festival is called A3C—All 3 Coasts—one of the largest hip-hop festivals and conferences in the United States. I sat front row at a one-on-one conversation between Marc Lamont Hill and Jeezy, and got to meet Keith Shocklee of Public Enemy. It was the kind of expe-

rience I craved from college, but didn't think I could get at St. Thomas until it happened. Life is full of surprises.

Snowbunnies

1. All my college friends who are currently in relationships, as well as myself, are with women of color. Ha!

Sociology

1. Lyor Cohen currently oversees 300 Entertainment. Notable artists on 300's roster include Fetty Wap, Young Thug, Tee Grizzley, and Migos. He's a great executive, also, an Israeli-American man who shepherds the careers of many young Black men who come from no money. My problem isn't with Cohen; it's the pattern of wealthy White men pulling the strings of Black creatives that concerns me.

2. Chief Keef also failed to sell as many units of his debut album *Finally Rich* as he was expected to. That being said, his experimental approach to music and the constant troubles of his personal life were still major factors in Interscope's decision to drop him.

3. I was going to give the Chair a proper pseudonym, but "the Chair" grew on me as a funny yet formidable identity.

GRAD School

1. Johnny gave me this detail along with the rest of the story of his first encounter with Miss Vivian.

The African Apartments

1. Personal experience. Had a roommate try to guilt me into paying him for several snacks I had over the course of the semester at the very end of that semester. The same kid also showed off $300 worth of silver coins he bought as a fun investment. Should have eaten more of his food.

2. I'd often get to a point in my conversations with Hughbert where I'd say something along the lines of, "I can't believe all the things you do are possible." His best response to my shock and awe was, "Man, it's *America.* There's *so much* crazy shit you can do."

Tweak

1. The ability to post anonymously on Yik Yak made it a great place for closeted racism at St. Thomas. It was frustrating to read trolling comments about on-campus racial justice protests, or the "overwhelming" presence of Black students, but at least it explicitly proved the existence of racial tension.

2. He literally couldn't stop laughing. He had this strained look in his eyes that indicated he was trying, but the weed was fucking him up. Five other people were there, watching in concern and disbelief. It was weird.

3. My episode actually happened half a year after Darrell's, but placing mine first in the chapter made more narrative sense. My troubles at St. Thomas weren't as great as Darrell's, and his breakdown had a backstory and

moments of action that were easier to visualize than the muddled trek through my subconscious.

Nigga

1. Just type "Today I got time cuz kid" into YouTube's search bar. You should be able to find several copies of the video. The original uploader of the video was a Black guy who claimed to be in the same set of Crips "Today I got time cuz" kid is/was in. The uploader's support, plus the nonchalant presence of the Black man standing in the video's backdrop, makes me think I'm not alone as a Black male thinking this White kid authentically owned 'nigga'. If it's not that deep to you, just watch for a quality minute of laughs.

Public Safety

1. Abeye and I cry laughing about that particular incident report to this day. Don't care, it's hilarious.

10 Deep

1. Much like "the Chair," "redheaded Bostonian Australian kid" is a title with way more character than a pseudonym like "Steve". Unsurprisingly, our Bostonian Aussie friend had quite the accent. He was also known for intentionally drinking cheap brown liquor and describing women in shockingly vulgar ways when he didn't like who he was talking about. Otherwise, a good dude. Left for Australia right after graduation, and I'll probably never hear from him again.

SDIS, Part 1

1. Once as an SDIS intern, Laura brought me to assist in an SDIS presentation to the Board of Trustees about the office's role on campus and its performance. One trustee, a White woman, led her feedback with a statement about how she was qualified to speak on the needs of students of color because she was, "funding one of them." She then went on to question if reserving resources specifically to support students of color was akin to racial segregation. The praise St. Thomas gave to its donors in the form of banquets, good press, and pushy requests for scholarship recipients to write "Thank You" letters to donors didn't feel right after seeing one in person.

SDIS, Part 2

1. It amazed me that a school fighting so hard to be seen as progressive while preserving its Catholic roots didn't do more to acknowledge the story of Father John Henry Dorsey earlier. The history of underrepresented people seems to always be at great risk of disappearing, even a story as unique as a Black man training to be a priest in Minnesota in 1888. I'm proud of Cory and the students that rallied around the petition, and as far as the Dorsey profile in the newsroom goes, better late than never.

Ball Is Not Life

1. We literally had to pause our game since half of us were on the floor laughing. He pretty much ran to the hoop without dribbling, *convinced* it was a legal move.

Facing a Bottle of Henny

1. The funny part about the central role Hennessy plays in
   this book is that cognac isn't even close to being my favorite type of alcohol. I'm much more likely to buy wine,
   saké, or a six-pack of IPA. Even if the choices are hard
   liquor, you can find me where the clear drank is at:
   Patrón, Grey Goose, Bacardi White Rum, Bombay,
   maaan. I'll even drink select whiskeys before I go for the
   'yac. But you can't beat holding a bottle of Henny, or
   looking at one, or taking pictures with one. And for a
   drink that's basically "burnt wine" (look up the etymolo-
   gy of 'brandy'), Hennessy is pretty smooth. I have great
   appreciation for it as a celebratory drink. Consuming it
   as casually as you would wine or beer would be an injustice, honestly.

About The Author

...

Alexander "Zander" Tsadwa (tSAHD-wuh or SAHD-wuh) is a perpetually bemused Ethiopian-American man. In his quest to be less confused by America, Zander serves as an independent culture broker, a writer and content manager at Across The Culture, and a speaker on multiculturalism, racial identity, and cross-cultural communication. In his downtime, Zander enjoys walking, journaling, and logging out of Twitter in fits of frustration. He also toys with the possibility of further complicating his professional life by releasing a bunch of music he wrote and recorded out of passion.

For more of Zander's writing, visit acrosstheculture.com.

Thoughts and questions about Zander or his work? Learn more at zandertsadwa.com, or hit him up @Zandersagwa on Twitter. If you got somethin' slick to say, know that Zander respectfully claps back.

Made in the USA
San Bernardino, CA
24 July 2018